What Will You Do with King Jesus?

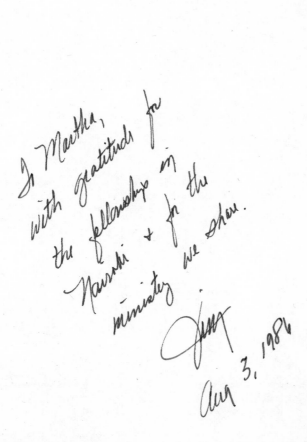

To Martha,
with gratitude for
the fellowship in
ministry we share.

Jim
Aug 3, 1986

What Will You Do with King Jesus?

Pictures of the Kingdom of God
in Matthew

James A. Harnish

THE UPPER ROOM
Nashville, Tennessee

What Will You Do with King Jesus?

Scripture quotations not otherwise identified are the author's paraphrase.

Scripture quotations designated RSV are from the Revised Standard Version of the Bible, copyrighted 1946, 1952, and © 1971 by the Division of Christian Education, National Council of the Churches of Christ in the United States of America, and are used by permission.

Scripture quotations designated TEV are from the *Good News Bible, The Bible in Today's English Version,* copyright by American Bible Society 1966, 1971, © 1976, and are used by permission.

Scripture quotations designated NEB are from *The New English Bible,* © The Delegates of the Oxford University Press and the Syndics of the Cambridge University Press 1961 and 1970, and are reprinted by permission.

Scripture quotations designated KJV are from the King James Version of the Bible.

We express appreciation to the publishers for allowing us to include quotations from the following works:

"The Road Not Taken" in THE POETRY OF ROBERT FROST edited by Edward Connery Lathem. Copyright 1916, © 1969 by Holt, Rinehart and Winston. Copyright 1944 by Robert Frost. Reprinted by permission of Holt, Rinehart and Winston, Publishers, the Estate of Robert Frost, and Jonathan Cape Limited, publishers in the United Kingdom.

THE HIDING PLACE by Corrie ten Boom with John and Elizabeth Sherrill. Published by Chosen Books Inc., Chappaqua, New York.

CHRIST IN THE CONCRETE CITY. Copyright 1960 by P. W. Turner. Copyright 1983 by P. W. Turner. Reprinted by permission of Baker's Plays, Boston, MA 02111.

Book Design: Linda Bryant
Cover Design: B. J. Osborne
Cover Transparency: Frances Dorris
First Printing: January, 1986 (7)
Library of Congress Catalog Card Number: 85-52013
ISBN: 0-8358-0530-1

Printed in the United States of America

For Carrie Lynn and Deborah Jeanne,
Lord, make them instruments of your peace

CONTENTS

FOREWORD

This is James Harnish's first book. I'm happy to have played a role in its publication, by encouraging him to write in the first place and by commending him to the publishers. I did this because I believe Jim is an outstanding communicator and has a message people need.

His genius, I believe, is at four points:

One, he begins where his readers are, at the point of their need, concern, and/or interest.

Two, he is able to take "old" truths and apply them relevantly to our daily lives.

Three, his metaphors, images, and illustrations are fresh and lively—the reader can identify.

Four, he is clear, and his language is precise. There is no fuzziness about what he means.

It was said of Jesus, "The common people heard him gladly" (Mark 12:37, KJV). I believe that any people who are interested in help for their lives and want to grapple with the Christian message will hear Jim Harnish gladly.

The book is a study of the Gospel of Matthew from the perspective of "pictures of the kingdom of God." Don't let that throw you. The kingdom of God is one of the biggest and most important ideas in the Bible and Christian thought. This study is sound in terms of scholarship, but it is not "scholarly" in the sense of being technical or aloof. It is where we live. You will profit from reading it personally, and, even more, you will be enriched by sharing it as a study with friends.

This is Jim's first book, but I predict it will not be his last. His way of communicating and the gospel to which he is committed are desperately needed by all of us.

MAXIE D. DUNNAM

PREFACE

Once when I was visiting in another church, I noticed a plaque, clearly meant to be seen from the pulpit, which quoted words from the Gospel of John (12:21, KJV): "Sir, we would see Jesus."

It is truly exciting and demanding to find ways to help people see Jesus—see him not only in the Gospels, but in the ordinary experiences of their own lives as well. The dual purpose of this book is to help us see Jesus as Matthew portrayed him, but also to see him in the real world in which we live. My highest hope is that somewhere in these chapters you will be brought into contact with the living presence of the One whom Matthew so powerfully described.

The majority of my own discoveries in faith have been in fellowship with a few trusted Christian friends. To that end, each chapter is followed by suggestions for reflection and discussion. It is my hope that this book will be a helpful resource for study, prayer, sharing groups.

I would like to express my appreciation to the people of St. Luke's United Methodist Church, who first heard this material in sermon form and who have helped shape it in more ways than they could possibly imagine; to Jo Sattelmeier, my friend and colaborer in the gospel (I now understand why most authors begin by thanking their secretaries!); to Dr. Dan Johnson, soul friend and biblical scholar, who read the manuscript and made many honest and helpful suggestions; and to Maxie Dunnam, encourager extraordinary.

Orlando, Florida
Holy Week, 1985

INTRODUCTION

Listen to the Music

The title of the book is simply *Karsh*. You will recognize it by the eye-catching cover picture of Sophia Loren wearing a large red hat. Yousuf Karsh is recognized as the premiere portrait photographer of our time. The book which bears his name is a collection of 185 famous faces from Franklin Roosevelt to Ronald Reagan, from Pope John XXIII to Andy Warhol, from Bette Davis to Helen Keller. The only portrait Karsh ever took of a person's back was taken of Pablo Casals, the exiled Spanish cellist, in a small French abbey in 1954. Karsh writes that as he was setting up his equipment Casals began playing Bach on his cello. Karsh was so enthralled by the music that he almost forgot why he was there. He took his portrait of Casals as a little bald-headed man bent over his cello, frozen in time against the plain stone wall of that chapel.

Years later, when the portrait was on exhibition in the Museum of Fine Arts in Boston, another old, bald-headed man came day after day to stand for long periods of time in front of the portrait. The curator of the museum noticed him and, when his curiosity finally got the best of him, went over, tapped the little man on the shoulder, and asked why he stood so long before the portrait. The old man, with obvious irritation, turned on the curator and said, "Hush, young man, hush—can't you see I'm listening to the music!"

Karsh watched Casals play Bach and preserved the image in a picture. The old man, looking at the picture, could hear the music. This is the process by which I want to approach the Gospels. The Gospel writers, like Karsh, were artists who saw, heard, experienced Jesus and presented a picture. You and I, looking at that picture, are invited to hear the music, to see and feel the presence of God in Jesus Christ.

This book is not a commentary on Matthew; there is a wide assortment of commentaries available today by scholars more able than I. Rather, this book is simply a collection of word pictures, family snapshots, museum pieces which grew out of my own attempt to hear the music of Matthew's Gospel in the tempo of my own times.

In his novel *The Clowns of God*, Morris West has Jean Marie, a former pope, say, "The biggest mistake we've all made through the ages is to try to explain the ways of God to men. We shouldn't do that. We should just announce Him. He explains himself very well!"

The goal of this book is not to explain the ways of God to humankind, but simply to announce God's way revealed in Jesus Christ, to point out the pictures of Jesus that Matthew has hung on the wall for us, and then to allow the living Christ to "explain himself" in our individual experiences.

Karsh observed Casals playing Bach and presented a picture. A nameless old man, looking at the picture, could hear the music. Matthew observed Jesus Christ and presented his picture. My highest hope is that by looking into these portraits we may catch the music of his spirit likewise.

1

The Child Born to Be King

Read: Matthew 1–2

Some things never change. I remember the day my daughter's first book report was due in seventh grade. I discovered that English teachers ask the same questions today they asked when I was her age. One of them is: Who are the main characters in the story?

If you ask that question about the opening chapters of the Gospel according to Matthew, you will probably be surprised with the answer, particularly if you are accustomed to the Christmas story as told by Luke, sung in carols, and painted on Christmas cards. Mary and Joseph are in both stories, but where Luke gives center stage to Mary, Matthew focuses the spotlight on Joseph. Futhermore, at the center of the Matthew's action is Herod, the vicious, corrupt, conniving, murderous puppet king of Judea. Other major characters include those nameless strangers who came from the East searching for the newborn King of the Jews. Were they wise men? Astrologers? Kings?

Matthew's account also differs from Luke's in color, in texture, and in mood. Luke's narrative is filled with light, music, and joy. Matthew's feels shadowy, dark, heavy. Seeing the difference, I began asking Matthew some very tough questions: Why are the familiar scenes left out? Why no shepherds? Why no angels singing, "Glory to God in the highest, peace on earth, goodwill, to men" (Luke 2:14)? Why no crowded inn or manger?

I asked some equally difficult questions about what Matthew presents instead. Why give center stage to Herod of all people? Why so much emphasis on his deceit and trickery? Why follow these visitors from the East? We do not know their names, where they came from, where they went. We do not even know how many there were, in spite of all the carols, paintings, and legends about the three kings. And why clutter the story with the gory slaughter of Bethlehem's little boys?

Frankly, it seemed a strange way to begin the Gospel. But I soon discovered the underlying reason Matthew does it. The drama of Herod and the Wise Men, the king in Judea and the kings from the East, is the frame through which Matthew wants us to view the whole story of Jesus. It sets the theme, the tone, the direction for everything that follows. The "good news" for Matthew is simply this: The King has come! This Jesus, son of Joseph, born in Bethlehem while Herod ruled Jerusalem, is in fact the child born to be King—the real King, the true King, the King of Kings and the Lord of Lords.

February 22, 1972. March 1, 1974. The dates on which my daughters were born are carved in my memory. I felt as if all of creation was waiting for me to announce their arrival. You can imagine my surprise when I realized that most of the world went right along as if nothing was happening.

By contrast, do you remember the birth of Britain's Prince William? The whole world followed Diana through her pregnancy. When Charles announced the birth, Britain celebrated and the whole world took notice. Why? Because William is the future king. He stands in the royal line. He is the child born to be king.

When you sit down to read Matthew, it may help if you keep this idea of royalty in mind. The first thing Matthew does is give us a long, boring list of the ancestors of Jesus. To us they are strangers with almost unpronounceable names. It is almost enough to make us give up before chapter 2! But Matthew knows the audience he intends to reach. This is an audience made up mostly of Jews. He is demonstrating that Jesus did not simply come out of nowhere. Jesus is in the line of God's covenant; he comes out of the history of the faith. He is not an imposter who takes the throne by force, power, or deceit, the way Herod did; he is in the line, he is the rightful King. That is also why Matthew emphasizes Joseph and skips over Mary. The list has almost nothing to do with biology and everything to do with theology, almost nothing to do with genetics and everything to do with faith.

The primary purpose of this Gospel is to announce the coming of the kingdom of God; the rule, authority, will, and way of God worked out in human life and history. Its bold affirmation is that God's kingdom comes not in ideas, not in power, not in proclamations or military might, but in a baby born in Bethlehem, a child born to be King. Matthew says, "Look at his life, listen to his words, catch the feeling of his compassion and the power of his love, be controlled by his spirit and then you'll know what it means to live under the rule of God, to be a part of God's kingdom."

Our familiarity with the story probably keeps us from experiencing the suspense which surrounds the moment when the Wise Men enter Herod's court asking, "Where is the child who is born to be king of the Jews?" (2:2, NEB).

Herod was no fool. He knew what it takes to make it to the top. Even more, he knew what it takes to stay there. If he suspected that someone was a threat to his power and authority, he had them eliminated. By the time he was finished, he had murdered one of his wives, his three eldest sons, and a brother-in-law. It is said that even Augustus, the Roman Emperor, once commented it was safer to be Herod's pig than to be Herod's son.

Herod knew he had only two alternatives when faced with an upstart king: either to recognize, honor, and obey him or to fear, reject, and destroy him. Herod made his choice and Matthew records it in all its cruel brutality: "[Herod] was furious. He gave orders to kill all the boys in Bethlehem and its neighborhood who were two years old and younger" (2:16, TEV). Matthew hangs the gruesome picture out as evidence of what Herod would do in his attempt to reject this child and protect himself.

As a stark contrast, Matthew holds up the picture of the mysterious visitors from the East. Herod experienced fear, but they experienced joy. Herod set out to destroy the child; they went off to worship him. Herod marked the date of his birth with blood; they celebrated it with gifts of gold, frankincense, and myrrh. Herod attempted to destroy the child; they knelt down to worship him.

It is as if Matthew is saying to us, "Take your choice. What will you do? How will you respond to the child born to be King?" The silent struggle involved in this choice is like a great underground river, an undercurrent beneath everything else that Matthew records.

In chapter 3 we will hear John the Baptist say,

"There is one coming who is greater than I. I am not worthy even to unlatch his sandles" (v. 11).

In chapter 4 we will see Jesus struggle with Satan, who tempts him by saying, "Come worship me and I will give you the whole world." "Go away!" Jesus answers, "You shall worship the Lord your God and him only will you serve" (vv. 9–10).

In the Sermon on the Mount we will be taught to pray, "Thy kingdom come, / Thy will be done, / On earth as it is in heaven" (6:10, RSV).

We will hear Jesus say:

"He who is not with me is against me" (12:30, RSV).

"Whoever loves even his father and mother more than he loves God is not fit for the Kingdom" (10:37).

"No one can serve two masters; for either he will hate the one and love the other, or he will be devoted to the one and despise the other. You cannot serve both God and [money]" (6:24, RSV).

At the climax of the story, another ruler, Pilate, will push Jesus into the judgment hall of history with these words: "What will you do with Jesus who is called the Messiah, the King?" (27:22).

Jesus will die with these words over his head: "This is Jesus the King of the Jews" (27:37, RSV).

And, finally, the disciples will hear the risen Christ say, "All authority in heaven and on earth has been given to me" (28:18, RSV).

Make no mistake about it: Matthew is a tough Gospel. The words of compassion and peace, the moments of healing and joy are there. But flowing underneath the entire story is this disturbing dilemma: What will you do with the child born to be King? Will you find and worship him with the Wise Men, or will you reject and crucify him with Herod?

One of my favorite television shows of recent

years is the PBS series "Upstairs, Downstairs." The story is set in England, just after the turn of the century. Upstairs are the Bellamy's, one of the aristocratic families of London. Downstairs are the cooks, maids, and butlers, who, in British terms, were "in service." In one episode, an impetuous young servant, filled with his own importance, tells Hudson, the head butler, that he is tired of "service." He wants to live his life his own way. And besides, he complains, his master is a fool.

As I remember, Hudson replies, "So, you serve a fool. I serve a man who is gentle and brave, a family which is good and noble. I am proud to be in his service." Then, in a typically British and very fatherly way, he concludes, "After all, we all say 'Sir' to someone; all except King George."

We all say "Sir" to someone or something, to some motivating, driving authority in our lives. Matthew places before us a great affirmation: The King has come! The true King, the rightful King, the one who reveals to us the kingdom of God. But he also confronts us with a disturbing dilemma: Whom will you serve? What will you do with this child born to be King?

Living into the Story
Suggestions for Reflection and Discussion

1. If you had never heard the Christmas story and had only this account of the birth of Jesus, how would you respond?

2. What surprised you the most as you read Matthew's account of Jesus' birth?

3. Can you identify with one of the main characters in the story? How would you feel if you were Herod?

The Wise Men? Mary? Joseph? The mothers in Bethlehem?

4. "We all say 'Sir' to someone or something." What is the practical authority for your life today? Who or what defines the operating assumptions that underlie your attitudes, values, and behavior?

2

What's He Doing Here?

Read: Matthew 3:1–12

The setting was the lavish "Ballroom of the
Americas" at Walt Disney World's Contemporary
Resort Hotel. The event, a black-tie fund-raiser for the
USO. The featured guest, Bob Hope. It was, to say the
least, one of the major social events of the season. I
would have had little hope of attending had it not
been for the graciousness of friends. I was doing my
best to fit in with a very sophisticated, well-dressed
crowd, when I met someone I knew on the hotel staff.
Obviously surprised to see me, she blurted out,
"What are you doing here?"

"What are you doing here?" As you read
through the Gospel, you may be tempted to ask that
question of John the Baptist. The rugged prophet of
the wilderness, with his camel's hair cloak on his
back, his leather belt around his waist, the locusts
and wild honey still dripping from his lips, hardly
seems appropriate. I am often tempted to ask, "Who
invited him? What's he doing here?"

Even more obtrusive than John's appearance,
however, is his preaching. Some biblical characters

are clearly in the story to comfort the afflicted. John, on the other hand, is clearly here to afflict the comfortable. His words are like fingernails scratching on a blackboard. His call to repentance is like a wire brush scraping the barnacles from the hull of our soul. He punctures our pretentions, shatters our sophisticated facades, cuts through all our smoke screens, and forces us to deal with exactly who and what we are.

Most of us have experienced a John the Baptist in our own lives. Sooner or later we run into someone who shatters the illusion we have so carefully built around ourselves, someone who strips away our defense mechanisms and forces us to examine the things that motivate and drive us. Perhaps John described himself best when he said that he was "the axe . . . laid to the root of the trees" (3:10, RSV).

I discovered the power of this metaphor shortly after my family and I purchased a small home on the shore of a beautiful lake in northern Florida. No one had lived in the house for over a year, and nature had taken control. Down at the lakefront, right beside the dock, a massive bramblebush had grown. Its long, twisting vines totally engulfed the earthbound end of the dock. It was not possible to get past the bush and onto the dock without being snagged by its thorns.

On our first trip to the lake, we cut the brambles back just enough to get onto the dock. Finally, however, we could no longer postpone the inevitable task of cutting it back. We took the clippers, ax, and hatchet and began to cut the bramblebush down to the ground. When we finally reached the ground, we discovered the most awesome root system I had ever seen. We hacked, chopped, and dug it out until we had cleared away as much as we could. Now, however, several years later, I know that some of those roots are still there. If I don't take the ax back to it now and then, it will return, trying to regain control of the shoreline.

My labor over that bramblebush helped me to experience an analogy for the witness of John the Baptist in my own journey of faith. He comes to clear the path, to straighten the road, to prepare the way for the coming of the kingdom of God. He is the ax laid to the roots of who I am, what I value, where I am headed in my life.

Matthew paints a clear picture of this process in John's conflict with the Sadducees and Pharisees. They were the religious leaders of the day. They thought they had all the answers. In fact, their full-time occupation was to keep the rest of the world in proper order until the Messiah could come to take over. But when John sees them standing in the crowd, he goes on the attack. "You brood of vipers! You snakes!" he calls. Then he lays his ax to the taproot, the core of who and what they are. "Don't think you are going to escape God's judgment by saying, 'We are the sons of Abraham.'" They were the sons of Abraham—that's how they got their jobs. They were in the line, they had the right blood, and they were proud of it! But John cuts directly across the grain of that pride by saying, "God can take rocks out of the river and make better sons than you!" John is not nearly as concerned about their ancestry as he is their loyalty to the kingdom, not nearly as concerned about their "fathers" as about their "King." He knows that they are most likely to keep from responding to the kingdom of God in the future because of their pride and loyalty to the past. The ax must be laid to that root before they will be free to follow the new King. It's a tough word John the Baptist has for us, a word that cuts through the tangled maze of our deepest values, the things that motivate and drive us, and gets down to who and what we really are. John is saying that when the kingdom of God comes it will require a radical reordering of our priorities, a change of our ultimate loyalties, a redirecting of our energy and commitments. He points to the things we value most and forces us to ask if they might be the very things which stand in the way of our loyalty to God's kingdom.

It would be comfortable if we could dismiss him by saying, "Well, that's John the Baptist for you. Live out in the desert, eat those locusts and wild honey, and pretty soon you'd go crazy, too!" But Matthew will not let us off the hook that easily. In chapter 19, verses 16 through 24, he records the story of the rich, young ruler. This man has everything going for him. He is rich, young, and he obviously has authority and power. He is probably everybody's "most likely to succeed." He asks Jesus, "What do I have to do to inherit eternal life?" What do I have to do to get ahold of the life I see in you? What do I have to do to be a part of God's kingdom?

Jesus replies very simply, "Keep the commandments God gave you if you want to enter life" to which the young man responds, "I've kept all of those from my youth." He had heard this before. He had tried to live by the rules, to do everything right, and had come up empty and dry. His life has all the zing of a wet tennis ball. He is still hungry for real life. He continues, "What else should I be doing?"

Then Jesus starts, "If you really want to become perfect . . ." That word, *perfect*, is important to Matthew. It means "complete" or "whole." Here it refers to life that is completely and wholly under the rule of God. Jesus says, "If you would like to be a complete person, if you would like to be a whole person, if you would like to be a person who lives under the kingdom of God, then go, sell all that you have and give the money to the poor. You will have riches in heaven. Then come and follow me."

Matthew records that the young man was the first of a long line who heard this message and sadly left it behind because of riches. Making the situation even more grim, Matthew follows with these words from Jesus: "I repeat: it is much harder for a rich person to enter the Kingdom of God than for a camel to go through the eye of a needle" (19:24, TEV).

The disciples ask, "Jesus, what's the point?" and we would ask the same thing. Jesus is not saying that every Christian has to take a vow of poverty. Jesus is instead laying the ax of love to the root of what motivates this young man. He can see that the man's loyalty to his wealth is more important than loyalty to God. The problem is not that he has riches but that his riches have him. He is so imprisoned by his wealth that he is not free to follow Christ.

The warning from John to the Pharisees and Sadducees and from Jesus to the rich young man is the same warning to us: The kingdom of God will require a reordering of what we consider important in life. The spirit of God will go directly to the taproot, which motivates and drives your life and mine. For the Sadducees and Pharisees, it was pride in their ancestral traditions. For the rich young man it was wealth. I wonder what it is for you and me? I wonder what it is in your life and in mine that blocks the coming of God's kingdom? I wonder what it is that keeps us from being free to follow Jesus Christ.

My brother spent a recent summer in England on a World Methodist Council exchange. He visited Epworth, the home of John and Charles Wesley, where he bought an 1876 book of Wesley hymns for me. As a part of my own spiritual discipline, I began praying my way through that hymnal, using those words to guide my meditation. I was immediately reminded of the importance Wesley and the early Methodists gave to the idea of "Christian perfection," the total surrender of a person's life to the rule of God. You hear it in these lines from a German hymn translated by John Wesley:

Is there a thing beneath the sun
That strives with Thee my heart to share?
Ah, tear it thence, and reign alone,
The Lord of every motion there!
Then shall my heart from earth be free,
When it hath found repose in Thee.

John the Baptist is present in the four Gospels and in your life and mine to lay the ax of divine love against the roots of our personalities, to set us free from anything that blocks our obedience to Christ, and to prepare the way for the coming of the kingdom of God in our world and our lives.

Living into the Story
Suggestions for Reflection and Discussion

1. Who has been a John the Baptist in your life, challenging your motivations and shattering your carefully constructed facade?

2. If you had been there, how would you have responded to the preaching of John the Baptist?

3. List two or three of the most important commitments of your life. What are the things which motivate you most strongly?

4. The problem for the religious leaders was pride; for the young man, wealth. Be as honest with yourself as possible. What could be the one thing which stands in the way of the coming of God's kingdom in your life?

5. For your meditation use the words translated by Wesley ("Is there a thing beneath the sun . . . "). What would it mean for you to live out that prayer in your life?

3

Hooked by the Divine Fisherman

Read: Matthew 4:12–22

Our journey through Matthew comes to a turning point at chapter 4, verse 17. Matthew records that after Jesus heard that John had been arrested, he "began to preach, saying, 'Repent, for the kingdom of heaven is at hand'" (RSV). This is exactly the same message John had been preaching, and exactly the same message Jesus will give his disciples to preach when he sends them out in chapter 10. These are not unconnected pieces of a confusing puzzle. John, Jesus, the disciples, and we, in our time, stand in the same line, hear the same call, respond to the same challenge: Repent, turn in a new direction—the kingdom, the rule of God, is near.

Thus, Jesus begins his own ministry. The first thing he does is recruit helpers. His first recruits are four fishermen, catching fish and mending their nets along the shore of the Sea of Galilee.

The best fish story I have ever heard comes from a novel by an Oregon fisherman, David Duncan, entitled *The River Why*. It is the story of Gus, another fisherman. Searching and restless, Gus is trying to find something to make sense out of his life. He has a friend, also a fisherman, named Nick, who has a calm serenity, an inner peace. Gus envies this and would like to find it for himself. He also notices that Nick has a long, red scar in the palm of his hand. Sitting by the fire one night, he summons the courage to ask Nick how he got that scar. Nick tells him his story.

He was on a minesweeper in the North Sea during the Second World War. He was an atheist and argued constantly with the Navy chaplain about the possibility of there being a just God in a world like this. One night the ship struck a mine off the coast of Norway and sank quickly. Half the crew died in their sleep, trapped beneath the deck. Nick was thrown into the icy sea. He described what happened in this way:

> From the top of the next swell I saw a big trawler bearing down on us. . . . [The man on the deck was] bellowin' at me and pointin' to a fishin' pole he had in his hand. . . . He cast over my head, but the line fell right on top of me. I tried to grab it . . . but I couldn't feel. . . . I watched the line runnin' through my hands as the boat moved off. . . . I came to the end of the line. There was a big ring of cork tied to it. I took the cork into my hand again . . . tried to curl my body around it, tried to make it a part of me—and that's when I saw it.

Nick reached inside his shirt and pulled a heavy gauge, black, five-inch fishhook, which he carried on a chain around his neck. Gus knew how the story would end.

> I knew what hooks were for. . . . I tried to trap my wrist in the crook—but as you can see, it's too small. The boat was atop the next crest. It was my last chance. I took the hook, held the point, steady as I could, right against the palm of my hand. . . . The trawler disap-

peared over the wave. A pain shot up my arm. I was dragged over, then under the water. I began to drown. . . . I awoke in the galley of the trawler, pukin' up water.

He stopped his story there, turned to Gus and said:

I tell you, Gus, I was right about God. He isn't just. If He was, I'd have sunk there in my North Sea stupidity. But thank God He's more than just. . . . I don't know how to put it. I'm still not religious. . . . But since this hook pierced me the world hasn't been the same. I just didn't know anything, nothing at all, till God let me watch that line run away from me, my hands all powerless an' cold. You're young, Gus. I don't know if you've been to that place beyond help or hope. But I was there. . . . And I was sent the help unlooked for, an' it came in the shape of a hook. Nothin' will ever be the way it was before that day, not for me.

And then Nick stretched his hand toward Gus and opened it, the scar red in the firelight.

"Behold son," he whispered. "Behold the sign of the Fisher's love for a wooden-headed ass."

Something like this happens in the lives of the fishermen Jesus meets. Simon Peter and Andrew are casting their nets, James and John, mending theirs. It is their work, their livelihood, their occupation, but not their calling. One day Jesus comes along the seashore, calling to them, "Come, follow me, and I will make you more than fishermen; I will make you fishers of men."

He gets his hook into their souls, and at great risk, probably not completely sure what they are doing or why, they grab onto that hook, leave everything—nets, ships, even father—and follow him. And nothing will ever be quite the same again, nothing the way it was before. Not for them, and not for us either.

The same thing happens in chapter 9 when the author writes himself into the drama, the way Alfred Hitchcock used to write himself into each of his movies. Jesus passes by a tax collector's table where a man named Matthew is doing his job, collecting the taxes. Again he says, "Come, follow me," and Matthew gets up to follow (v. 9).

Interesting, isn't it. Jesus calls them while they are at work, the place where they made their living, their occupation. They find "the help unlooked for," which came in the hook of divine grace. Nothing will ever be the same again.

Two things fascinate me about these stories. The first is the simplicity of the call. Jesus asks only one thing, "Will you follow me?" There is no application for employment, no interview, no analysis of strengths and weaknesses, no test of dogma or tradition, no initation exercise. He issues only a simple invitation: "Follow me. Let me take what you have and I will use it in ways you could never imagine. Come, follow me."

There was a time when I thought a pastor's responsibility was to make sure that everyone who joined the church had a clear understanding of theology, had given full consideration to all the implications of their commitment, had basically become comfortable in the ideas of their faith. But now I am in a community filled with unchurched people. I serve in a church that is attempting to reach and touch men and women who have had very little formal religious training. Many of them feel that at some point in their lives, they became alienated from "organized religion." In this setting I am rediscovering the power of the personality of Jesus Christ to draw, lure, entice men and women into discipleship. I am falling back on that simple, clear invitation to follow him.

Each Friday morning I meet with several other men for breakfast. One book we have discussed is Leslie Weatherhead's *The Christian Agnostic*. Weatherhead defines a "Christian agnostic" as "a person who is immensely attracted by Christ and who seeks to show his spirit, to meet the challenges, hardships and sorrows of life in the light of that spirit, but who, though he is sure of many Christian truths, feels that he cannot honestly and conscientiously 'sign on the dotted line' that he believes certain theological ideas about which some branches of the church dogmatize."

He invites people to follow Christ, "to listen, to consider, to pray, to follow, and ultimately to believe only those convictions about which the experience of fellowship made him sure."

He suggests that we leave other, more uncomfortable ideas in a mental box labeled "Awaiting Further Light," accepting them only as they begin to become real for us.

Weatherhead's approach has had an amazing, liberating effect on our group. We have become free to say, "I'm not sure I believe that," while still allowing ourselves to say, "I am a Christian, a follower of Jesus Christ." It has allowed us to be honest and free with each other in our search for a meaningful faith.

This approach is also consistent with the amazing simplicity of the call Jesus offered his first disciples. It is a call to which many of us can respond, even if we cannot fully respond to all of the theological tests and traditions which have grown around it.

I am fascinated with the simplicity of the fishermen's response. There is something so enticing, so alluring, so mysteriously challenging about this man of Nazareth, that these men, caught up in the busyness of their daily work, are willing to lay it all aside to rise up and follow him. There is little emotion and very little doubt, just a deep, inner awareness that if there is anyone worth following, it is this man, who said, "Follow me."

To be sure, things would soon become very complicated! Following Jesus meant that they would be led out of the mundane, ordinary, predictable world of their nets and boats and into the risky, dangerous, unpredictable world that we call Christian discipleship. In one sense, Jesus will complicate their lives immensely, causing them to think things they had never thought, act in ways they had never acted, care about people for whom they had never cared. Nothing would ever be the same again. But at the heart of it all is a very simple, clear response to a very simple, clear invitation. They choose to follow Jesus and the rest is history.

One of the turning points in World War II was the Battle of the Bulge. It was really a multitude of smaller battles, fought out along the Allied lines. In *World War II*, James Jones describes it: "No one of these little road junction stands could have had a profound effect on the German drive. But hundred of them, impromptu little battles at nameless bridges and unknown crossroads, had an effect of slowing enormously the German impetus. . . . These little diehard 'one-man-stands,' alone in the snow and fog without communications, would prove enormously effective out of all proportion to their size."

"Enormously effective out of all proportion to their size." Peter, Andrew, James, John, and Matthew were ordinary men, doing their ordinary tasks. No one of them could change the world, no one of them could bring in the kingdom of God, but they, and hundreds like them across the past two thousand years, have been "enormously effective out of all proportion to their size." Jesus hooked these ordinary people and used them in very extraordinary ways.

The same invitation comes to you and me today. Jesus meets us in the common patterns of our lives and says, "Come, follow me. Give me your talents, your skills, your hands, your wealth, your energy, and I will use them to heal the sick, to raise the dead, to cleanse, to liberate, to free. Come, follow me, and I will use you as part of the coming of the kingdom of God."

One of the heroes of the Christian faith in the twentieth century is Albert Schweitzer. Best known as a medical doctor, he was also a musician, theologian, and poet. In his book, *The Quest for the Historical Jesus*, Schweitzer wrote these familiar words which describe the simplicity of Jesus' call and of our response:

> He comes to us as One unknown, without a name, as of old, by the lakeside. He came to those men who knew him not. He speaks to us the same word: "Follow thou me!" and sets us to the tasks which He has to fulfill for our time. He commands. And to those who obey Him, whether they be wise or simple, He will reveal Himself in the toils, the conflicts, the sufferings which they shall pass through in his fellowship, and, as an ineffable mystery, they shall learn in their own experience who He is.

Nick was right. God isn't just. "He's more than just. . . . Behold the sign of the Fisher's love for a wooden-headed ass."

Living into the Story
Suggestions for Reflection and Discussion

1. How do you respond to the image of Jesus "getting

his hook" into the souls of Peter, Andrew, James, and John? Have you ever experienced that "hook" in your own life?

2. How did you begin your journey of faith? Was it a response to the simplicity of the call, "Follow me"? Can you identify with the disciples in the simplicity of their response?

3. Have you ever felt that you might be a "Christian agnostic"? How did Weatherhead's advice to put your doubts in a mental box labeled "Awaiting Further Light" give you a sense of liberation?

4. Have you known Christian men or women who were "enormously effective out of all proportion to their size"? Who were they? How did they influence you?

5. Look again at Schweitzer's words, "He comes to us . . ." Use them as a focus for a time of silent meditation.

4

Citizens of the Kingdom—
Who They Are

Read: Matthew 5:1–16

As a Christmas gift one year, my in-laws gave me
the first volume of William Manchester's biography of
Winston Churchill. Manchester titles the book *The
Last Lion*, identifying Churchill as the last of those
aristocrats who ruled England when England ruled
the world.

Manchester goes into great detail to describe the
British colonies in India and Africa. The British trans-
ported their culture, their language, their lifestyle,
even their "gentlemen's clubs" to foreign soil halfway
around the world. They lived in a foreign land, but
they were still subjects of the British king or queen.
The natives of Bombay, India, or Salisbury, Rhodesia,
could see what it was like to live in England under the
rule of Queen Victoria simply by looking in on one of
the British clubs at teatime and by watching the way
these people lived. The natives would instantly know
what it looked like to live under the authority of the
queen.

I want to bring this same feeling to the Sermon
on the Mount. These chapters are the Technicolor

picture, the living portrait of what it means to be citizens of the kingdom, to live in the world as men and women who live under the authority and rule of God. It is the living picture of those who have chosen to be subjects of the King.

William Barclay calls this passage "the essence of the Christian way of life."

E. Stanley Jones says this is "the way a Christian will act . . . his working philosophy of life . . . the main moral content of the word 'Christian.' "

John Wesley calls it Christ's "divine institution which is the compleat art of happiness."

It is the Magna Charta of the kingdom, the inaugural address of the new administration, the Technicolor picture of life in the kingdom of God.

The interesting thing is that the Sermon on the Mount is not really a sermon at all, at least not in the way we think of sermons. It is certainly not a particular sermon preached to a particular audience gathered in a particular place at a particular time. When Matthew says, "He taught them" (v. 2, RSV), he uses the Greek imperfect tense, which describes a repeated, continuous action in the past. Matthew is saying, "This is what Jesus was continuously teaching them," the way my daughters say, "Oh, Daddy, you always say that!" or the way we look back and say, "Dad always used to say . . ." In these chapters, Matthew has drawn together what Jesus was always teaching his disciples about what it means to be citizens of the kingdom of God.

The "sermon" begins with that poetic passage we call the Beatitudes. "Blessed are the poor in spirit, for theirs is the kingdom of heaven" (v. 3, RSV).

This is beautiful and it sounds religious, but if most of us are honest, we haven't the foggiest idea what it means. If we were to go out on the street and ask people what it means to be blessed by God, they would probably tell us something like this: "My orange grove escaped the freeze." "The kids haven't caught the flu." "I just got a raise." "We're going to have a baby." To be blessed in our world means that we escape the bad stuff and win the goodies. If we escape pain and gain pleasure, we have been blessed.

Nothing could be further from the biblical meaning of the word. The word we translate "blessed" is the Greek word *makarios*, which means bliss, joy, or happiness that is not dependent on external circumstances. The Greeks used it to describe the island of Cyprus, which they called the "Blessed" or the "Blissful Isle." They thought Cyprus was so beautiful, so complete, that one could live there and never have to go beyond its coastline to experience perfect happiness.

When I apply this image to the Beatitudes, I end up with something like this: The first mark of the citizens of the kingdom is that they have a deep inner joy that is not dependent on external circumstances but that emerges from the depths of who and what they are—a joy which comes from knowing that they are part of the kingdom of God.

This understanding of being blessed is a striking contrast to the world around us. The world promises that we will be happy if we get rich—just look at how happy the game show winners are! But Jesus said, "Blessed, happy are the poor in spirit, those who know they are spiritually destitute, for they are the ones who can receive the kingdom of God."

The world says we will be happy if we brazenly go forward with what we want to do with no regard for what God expects. But Jesus said, "Blessed, joyful are those who mourn, for only those who know and regret the full extent of their sins can be comforted."

The world says we will be happy if we are powerful, strong, in control. But Jesus said, "Blessed, joyful are the meek, those with gentle strength, for they are the ones who can be trusted to inherit the earth."

The world says we will find happiness in selfish pleasure, greed, and hedonistic sexual gratification. If you don't believe that, take a look at the movie listings in the newspaper or watch the music videos on MTV. But Jesus said, "Blessed, happy are those who hunger and thirst to be right with God, for they are the only people God can satisfy."

The world says we will be happy if we get revenge, take our troubles out on everyone who has hurt us, get our pound of flesh. But Jesus said, "Blessed, happy are the merciful, those who have learned to forgive, for only those who forgive others will experience the forgiveness of God."

The world says we will be happy if we learn to manipulate people, use relationships to our own advantage, always look out for number one. But Jesus said, "Blessed, happy are those who have a pure heart, whose motives are clean and clear, for they are the ones who will see God."

The world says happiness and peace can be secured by force, by military strength, by "Mutually Assured Destruction." But Jesus said, "Blessed, happy are the peacemakers, for they will be known as children of God."

The world says that happiness comes by avoiding suffering at all costs, compromising for the sake of comfort. But Jesus said, "Blessed, happy are those who are persecuted for doing God's work, for they will be given God's kingdom.

The world says happiness comes by having everyone like you, by winning everyone's praise. But Jesus said, "Blessed, happy are you when people insult you and persecute you and say all kinds of evil against you falsely for my sake. You will be rewarded. God's prophets have always been treated unfairly."

G. K. Chesterton said that the first time we read these words we feel that Jesus is turning everything upside down. He is! He challenges all the suppositions upon which so much of our world is built. But then, Chesterton said, we read it again and begin to feel that everything is actually rightside up. There is something in us which says, "Ah, this is life as God intended it to be lived!"

Arturo Toscanini was once the most famous orchestra conductor in the United States. In 1931, during the days of radio, NBC invited Toscanini to conduct a concert tour of Latin America. The day came for the musicians, gathered from orchestras across the country, to begin rehearsal. It was a hot August afternoon, in an unair-conditioned rehearsal hall. They began rehearsing Beethoven's Sixth Symphony. These were professional musicians who knew the music. They knew where to come in and where to rest. They knew where they could get up and take a walk and still be back in time to come in on their part. But something happened when Toscanini began to direct. By the end of the first movement they could sense it. No one was daydreaming; all of them were intent on the music. They played it as if it were entirely new. They came to the final movement and, when the maestro laid down his baton, the members of the orchestra rose to their feet in applause. Toscanini stood there until the applause ceased. Then he said to the orchestra, "That isn't Toscanini, that's Beethoven. You just never heard him before."

When I see human life the way Jesus describes it here, something in me says, "That is really life, life as God intended it. We just never saw it before."

These blessed people named here really are the salt of the earth! They may be unknown, unseen, and insignificant, but they are the preservative that keeps the rest of the world from decay and rot. They give flavor and zest to living.

These blessed people really are the light of the world! They may only be one insignificant candle, but they give light to the entire house. When people in a dark world see the work of these citizens of the kingdom, the people give glory to God because they know there is still hope for this world!

This is who we are called to be as citizens of the kingdom of God. We may be amazed or surprised—that is exactly the response Matthew intended! The Beatitudes are not placid statements spoken softly. They are exclamations. We step out into the morning sun after a foggy night and exclaim, "Wow! Look at that sunshine!" We hear a great piece of music and come away exclaiming, "Wow! That's really Beethoven!" The Beatitudes are similar exclamations. They exclaim, "Wow! Look at the happiness of those who are citizens of the kingdom of God! This is really living; we just never saw it before!"

I remember one of Charles Schulz's Peanuts cartoons, which I read years ago and continue to pull out of my memory every now and then. In the first frame Lucy asks Charlie Brown if he has ever known anyone who was really happy. Before she can finish her sentence, Snoopy comes dancing into the frame. He dances and bounces his way across two frames of the cartoon strip. Finally, in the last frame, Lucy finishes her sentence with the words "and was still in their right mind?"

The good news is that these citizens of the kingdom, these people who live under the authority and rule of God, are really happy and are really in their right mind. Jesus is saying, "Oh, how blest are the citizens of the kingdom of God!"

Living into the Story
Suggestions for Reflection and Discussion

1. Have you ever considered the Christian life as a Technicolor picture or a living portrait of what it means to live under the authority and rule of God? If people looked at your life hoping to discover what it means to live under the rule of God, what would they see?

2. Compare several contemporary translations of the Beatitudes. How are they alike or different? What does it mean to you to be "blessed"?

3. Do you agree that at first glance these teachings of Jesus seem to turn everything upside down? How do they begin to turn life rightside up?

4. Which one of the Beatitudes speaks most directly to your spiritual journey right now? Why?

5. Have you known persons who "fleshed out" one or more of the Beatitudes in their own life? Who were they? How did they influence you?

5

Citizens of the Kingdom—
Relationships with Others

Read: Matthew 5:17–48

I might was well confess that I am having a tough time adjusting to metric. My daughters are learning it, my wife teaches it, but I still get confused. Going down the interstate recently, I saw one of the most encouraging signs I had seen in a long time. It said, "Speed Limit 88." I thought, *this is too good to be true*! I looked at my speedometer, thought about stomping down on the accelerator, and then saw the small print: KMH. It was a totally different standard of measurement than the one I was accustomed to using. It was a different way of measuring space and time. It was too good to be true.

The world sees the Sermon on the Mount the way I saw that sign. Jesus calls the citizens of the kingdom, the people who live under the authority and rule of the love of God, to live by a standard of measurement that is totally different from the world around them. He makes this crystal clear with a set of parallel contrasts.

"You've always heard . . . " Jesus tells us. We know what is the accepted, normal, predictable behavior. We know the mores and traditions of our society. They are what our mothers always told us, the rules of the road for human relationships, the basic standards of behavior we have learned from childhood. Obey the rules, we are told. Do just what has to be done to stay inside the boundaries of the law. And there is nothing wrong with doing that. Jesus says, "I haven't come to destroy that. I've come to fulfill it, to fill it full of meaning and life." The law is not bad; it is simply not good enough.

"You've always heard, but now I say to you . . . " No longer are the common rules of the road sufficient for human life and relationships. No longer can citizens of the kingdom be satisfied simply to stay within the boundaries of predictable, expected, appropriate behavior. Jesus says, "Unless your goodness exceeds that of the Pharisees, you're not even on the doorstep of the kingdom of heaven!"

"You've always heard you shouldn't commit murder." We still hear this. It's the law in most countries. But Jesus says, "If you're going to be in my kingdom, not only should you not murder, but if you hold anger in your heart, if you say to your brother, 'You good-for-nothing,' you'll be brought before the Council. If you call your brother a worthless fool you'll be in danger of the fires of hell." It's not enough to merely restrain ourselves from murder; the demands of the kingdom penetrate into our feelings, our attitudes, our emotions.

Jesus says, "You've always heard you should not commit adultery." In spite of the influence of the afternoon "soaps," "Dallas," "Falcon Crest," and others, we still maintain this law prohibiting adultery. But Jesus continues, "Now I tell you: anyone who looks at a woman and wants to possess her is guilty of committing adultery with her in his heart. So, if your right eye causes you to sin, take it out and throw it away! It is much better for you to lose a part of your body than to have your whole body thrown into hell" (vv. 28-29, TEV). Jesus is saying that it's not enough simply to refrain from adulterous sexual involvement with another human being. Citizens of the kingdom are just as concerned with inner faithfulness, the inner covenant of love, respect, and commitment.

Jesus lived in a male dominated society where men could easily cast out a wife and get rid of her. All they had to do was step out into the square, announce three times that she was divorced, give her a paper, and the divorce was complete. Jesus said to these citizens, "You've always heard that anyone who divorces his wife must give her a written statement of divorce, but now I say to you that marriage relationships are much deeper than that." He sweeps away any shallow, flippant attempt to treat divorce as a simple, legal process. This forces us today to view our relationships in human rather than legal terms, to face up to the sometimes painful consequences of our actions in dealing with others.

Jesus next suggests an idea that, if taken seriously, would slash across half the need for the legal profession in our world today. "You've heard you ought to make your vows before the Lord, but I say to you, don't swear to God at all. When you say, 'Yes,' it ought to mean 'yes,' when you say, 'No,' it ought to mean 'no.' Your word should be your bond."

Then, as if all this wasn't enough, he gets even tougher. "You have heard that it was said, 'An eye for an eye and a tooth for a tooth.' But now I tell you: do not take revenge on someone who wrongs you. If anyone slaps you on the right cheek, let him slap your left cheek, too. And if someone takes you to court to sue you for your shirt, let him have your coat as well. And if one of the occupation troops forces you to carry his pack one mile, carry it two miles. When someone asks you for something, give it to him; when someone wants to borrow something, lend it to him" (vv. 38-42, TEV). Paul reaffirms this perspective in his letter to Romans: "Do not be overcome by evil, but overcome evil with good" (12:21, RSV). It's not enough just to stay within the boundaries of "an eye for an eye and a tooth for a tooth." Citizens of the kingdom are called to an aggressive goodwill, to an offense of love.

"You've heard you should love your friends and hate your enemies, but I say, love your enemies, pray for those who persecute you, so you may become sons and daughters of your Father who is in heaven." Jesus has changed the rules and, in the last example, he is telling us why: so we may become the sons and daughters of God. Jesus goes on to explain: "God makes the sun to shine on both the good and the bad, and sends the rain on the just and unjust. If you only love those who love you, you're not doing anything more than the Scribes and Pharisees. If you only give respect to those who treat you with respect you're not doing anything more than the pagans; any sinner can do that!"

The citizens of the kingdom are called to a new standard of measurement, nothing more or less than the perfect love of God. Jesus leads us out of the details of the law and into the demands of love, out of legalism and into life. He says it is not enough simply to obey the rules of the road, we must demonstrate aggressive love. Jesus calls us to a level of human relationships that is foreign territory for most of us, a totally different standard of measurement than the one to which we are accustomed.

Every now and then we can catch a glimpse of this kind of love at work. When we see it, it stands out like a beacon, forcing us to share it with someone else. Do you remember the story of Corrie ten Boom? Corrie and her family were protecting Jews in Holland as the Nazis swept across Europe. The family was arrested and placed in a concentration camp where Corrie watched her father and her sister, Betsie, die. In her book, *The Hiding Place*, she recounts the agony, humiliation, and pain of that experience, but she also recounts the way God's love and grace sustained her through that difficult time.

After the war, Corrie ten Boom became a refugee moving across Europe, trying to bring reconciliation and healing to that broken continent. One scene from her book has stuck with me ever since I first read it. She wrote:

> It was at a church service in Munich that I saw him, the former S.S. man who had stood guard at the shower room door in the processing center at Ravensbruck. He was the first of our actual jailers that I had seen since that time. And suddenly it was all there—the roomful of mocking men, the heaps of clothing, Betsie's pain-blanched face.
>
> He came up to me as the church was emptying, beaming and bowing. "How grateful I am for your message, *Fraulein*," he said. "To think that, as you say, He has washed my sins away!"
>
> His hands was thrust out to shake mine. And I, who had preached so often to the people in Bloemendaal the need to forgive, kept my hand at my side.
>
> Even as the angry, vengeful thoughts boiled through me, I saw the sin of them. Jesus Christ had died for this man; was I going to ask for more? Lord Jesus, I prayed, forgive me and help me to forgive him.
>
> I tried to smile, I struggled to raise my hand. I could not. I felt nothing, not the slightest spark of warmth or charity. And so again I breathed a silent prayer. Jesus, I cannot forgive him. Give me Your forgiveness.

As I took his hand the most incredible thing happened. From my shoulder along my arm and through my hand a current seemed to pass from me to him, while into my heart sprang a love for this stranger that almost overwhelmed me.

And so I discovered that it is not on our forgiveness any more than on our goodness that the world's healing hinges, but on His. When He tells us to love our enemies, He gives, along with the command, the love itself.

How do we pick out the citizens of the kingdom? What is the evidence in your life and mine that we are followers of Jesus Christ? Jesus said this is the evidence: The standard for our human relationships is nothing more or less than the perfect love that we have received from God, who sends sun on the good and bad and rain on the just and unjust. By this we will know who are sons and daughters of God.

Living into the Story
Suggestions for Reflection and Discussion

1. How do you measure or define your responsibility in interpersonal relationships? What standard do you use?

2. List the contrast which Jesus outlines in Matthew 5:21-48. How is Jesus' position different than the common assumptions about relationships?

3. Have you known any persons who actually lived by the kind of principles Jesus outlines here? Share their story with your group.

4. What changes do you need to make if you measure your relationships on this scale?

6

Citizens of the Kingdom— Relationship with God

Read: Matthew 6:1–7:29

One of my all-time favorite lines from a movie comes from *The Four Seasons*. Carol Burnett asks, "Is this the fun part? Are we having fun yet?"

Looking back across this discussion of the Sermon on the Mount, someone may be tempted to ask, "Is this the 'religious' part? Have we come to the 'God part' yet?" It takes a while to get there, at least the way Matthew has drawn this material together.

The Sermon on the Mount tries to answer a very simple question: How can we pick out the Christians in the world? What are the identifying marks of those men and women who are citizens of the kingdom, who live under the rule and authority of the kingdom of God? In the beginning of the "sermon," we saw that the first mark is joy, a sense of inner blessedness that is not dependent on external circumstances but that emerges out of the depths of who we are as disciples of Jesus Christ.

The second identifying mark of citizens of the kingdom is in relationships with others. These relationships operate on a totally different standard of measurement than those of the rest of the world. Citizens of the kingdom are called to relate to others with nothing less than the perfect love which we have received from our heavenly Creator.

Finally, in chapters 6 and 7, Matthew gets around to the "God talk," the collection of Jesus' teachings that deal specifically with our relationship with God.

This section opens with a warning: "Beware of practicing your piety before men in order to be seen by them; for then you will have no reward from your Father who is in heaven" (6:1, RSV). It is obvious from what follows that Jesus assumes his followers will "practice their piety." He does not say, "*If* you pray"; he does not say, "*If* you give"; he does not say, "*If* you fast and practice spiritual discipline." He says, "*When* you pray . . . *when* you give . . . *when* you fast." He operates on the assumption that his followers *will* practice spiritual discipline in their relationship with God.

When I realized this, I had to ask if it was more than the Master had a right to assume. Consider the amount of encouraging, prodding, and pushing it takes for some of us to get around to prayer. Consider all of the handy-dandy, professionally packaged, star-studded programs it takes to encourage us to give. Consider how foreign the whole idea of fasting and spiritual discipline is to most of the Christians I know. When I take a realistic look at life around me, something inside says, "Wait a minute, Jesus, this may be too much to assume." But Jesus doesn't seem to worry about that. He simply says, "These citizens of the kingdom will be about the business of practicing their piety." But he adds the warning: "Watch out for your motivation. Beware of practicing your piety before men so that you will be seen by them." To make sure he is understood, Jesus lists some specific examples of what that looks like:

When you give alms, sound no trumpet before you, as
the hypocrites do in the synagogues and in the streets,
that they may be praised by men. Truly, I say to you,
they have received their reward. But when you give
alms, do not let your left hand know what your right
hand is doing, so that your alms may be in secret; and
your Father who sees in secret will reward you.

When you pray, you must not be like the hypocrites; for they love to stand and pray in the synagogues and at the street corners, that they may be
seen by men. Truly, I say to you, they have received
their reward. But when you pray, go into your room
and shut the door and pray to your Father who is in
secret; and your Father who sees in secret will reward
you.

In praying, do not heap up empty phrases, as the
Gentiles do; for they think that they will be heard for
their many words.

—Matthew 6:2–7, RSV

This means that we cannot measure spirituality
by how long and how loud a person prays. "Do not
be like them. Your Father already knows what you
need before you ask him. This, then, is how you
should pray: 'Our Father in heaven: / May your holy
name be honored; / may your Kingdom come, / may
your will be done on earth as it is in heaven'" (6:8–10,
TEV).

"When you fast," Jesus says, "do not look dis-
mal, like the hypocrites, for they disfigure their faces
that their fasting may be seen by men" (6:16, RSV).
There has always been that company of sour saints
who think they can prove how spiritual they are by
how miserable they look, people who, if their religion
has any joy in it, need to notify their faces! Jesus says,
"Anoint your head and wash your face, that your
fasting may not be seen by men but by your Father

who is in secret; and your Father who sees in secret will reward you" (6:17–18, RSV).

This all means that the unique relationship with God to which Jesus calls us is profoundly personal. It goes down into the deepest, darkest, most hidden closets of our souls. It is so profoundly personal that it moves us out of the realm of the abstract into the realm of the concrete. It moves us out of theoretical debate about God into God's revelation of exactly what moves and motivates us.

To illustrate this principle, Jesus uses three very practical pictures. First is a picture any investor would enjoy. "Do not lay up for yourselves treasures on earth, where moth and rust consume and where thieves break in and steal, but lay up for yourselves treasures in heaven. . . . For where your treasure is, there will your heart be also" (6:19–21, RSV). This picture is almost self-explanatory. What gets our money gets us; where my treasure is, my heart will be also.

Next he uses a picture any optometrist would understand. "The eye is the lamp of the body" (6:22, RSV). There is a perspective through which each of us sees reality and if that "eye" is healthy and clean, the entire person will be whole. But if the "eye" is dark and "grungy," the entire personality will be filled with darkness.

Third, in a day filled with masters and with slaves, he draws upon an image that also speaks to us in our day. "You cannot serve two masters. You'll love one and despise the other, be loyal to one and hate the other. You cannot serve both God and money." You cannot serve both the kingdom of God and the kingdom of this world. You cannot be loyal to God and at the same time be ultimately loyal to anything else. Jesus calls us into a relationship with God which is so profoundly personal that it changes the deepest loyalties of our lives.

This relationship with God is so personal that, while the God in whom we believe is still God, still the Maker and Sustainer of the universe, God is, at the same time, so personally and deeply experienced in the subjective realities of our life that we use the name "Father." In fact, in the original language Jesus uses a word equivilent not to "Father," but to "Daddy." This is just how intensely personal our relationship with God is.

The second emphasis in chapter 6 begins at verse 25. Jesus begins to follow up on what he has said, revealing the results of our relationship with God. Because your relationship with God is so personal, because you say not only "God" but "Father," "therefore I tell you, don't be anxious, worried, uptight about your life, about what you eat, about what you will put on." Come on, Jesus! Tell that to a group of junior high youth who are getting dressed for the Valentine dance! Tell that to business persons who are getting ready to make the biggest deal of their lives!

"Is not life more than food, and the body more than clothing? Look at the birds of the air: they neither sow nor reap nor gather into barns, and yet your heavenly Father feeds them. Are you not of more value than they? And which of you by being anxious can add one cubit to his span of life?" (6:25–27, RSV). The answer to this question is, obviously, none of us. Medical science has shown us that not only will our worry, anxiety, and fear add nothing to the length of life, it will, in fact, reduce it. "Why are you anxious about clothing? Consider the lilies of the field, how they grow; they neither toil nor spin; yet I tell you, even Soloman in all his glory was not arrayed like one of these. But if God so clothes the grass of the field, which today is alive and tomorrow is thrown into the oven, will he not much more clothe you, O men of little faith? Therefore do not be anxious, saying, 'What shall we eat?' or 'What shall we drink?' or 'What shall we wear?' For the Gentiles seek all these things; and your heavenly Father knows that you need them all. But seek first his kingdom and his righteousness, and all these things shall be yours as well" (6:28–33, RSV).

It sounds so beautiful and yet it can be so difficult to live. When I think about the anxious, uptight lives we lead, so worried over transitory things and so oblivious to eternal things, it reminds me of the second verse in that old hymn, "What a Friend We Have in Jesus."

> O what peace we often forfeit,
> O what needless pain we bear,
> All because we do not carry
> Everything to God in prayer!

I wonder if there is any way to measure the amount of needless pain, fear, and anxiety we pile upon ourselves? I wonder if there will ever be any way to measure the amount of mental, emotional, and physical illness and suffering we bring on ourselves because we have never learned that we have a loving God who cares for us; because we have never learned to trust that "God is great and God is good." I wonder what it will take for us to learn the kind of trust and live the kind of relationship that Jesus describes in this passage—a relationship of ultimate trust in the goodness and the love of God.

The final thing Jesus says in the Sermon on the Mount is that this relationship with God is also productive. Every manager knows there are some sales people who never quite reach their potential because they never expect to. We know that one of the fundamental realities of human life is that we will never accomplish or achieve anything more than what we expect to accomplish or achieve, except for those moments of "surprising grace" which break in upon us now and then. For the most part, we will not accomplish more than that for which we reach. The problem some of us face in our relationship with God is either that we don't expect anything to happen or that we wouldn't know what to expect if we did.

In the concluding verses of the "sermon," Jesus answers both of these needs. First, he says we can expect something. We can expect tangible, measureable results from this kind of relationship with God. He gives us a lesson in horticulture to describe it: We can identify a tree by the fruit hanging on its branches. "Are grapes gathered from thorns, or figs from thistles? . . . Every sound tree bears good fruit, but the bad tree bears evil fruit. A sound tree cannot bear evil fruit, nor can a bad tree bear good fruit. Every tree that does not bear good fruit is cut down and thrown into the fire. Thus you will know them by their fruits" (7:16–20, RSV). A growing, personal, trusting relationship with God should have tangible results. We can see these results in the fruit that it bears.

The second need Jesus answers is, what can we expect? There are some things I'm convinced we *can't* expect. We can't expect to be protected from all diseases. We can't expect to be safe from all risk and danger. We can't expect suddenly to be rich and successful. We can't expect the winning ticket in the Irish Sweepstakes or a gold medal at the Olympics just because we pray for it. Jesus said there are two things we can expect from this kind of relationship with God. The first one is life—life that is so alive it can never be put to death. John records Jesus as saying, "I came that they may have life, and have it abundantly" (John 10:10, RSV). This relates back to the parable of the narrow and the broad way, which Matthew records. Jesus says, "There is a broad way that leads to destruction, there is a narrow way that leads to life." We can take our pick.

One of the local television stations recently did a special series of news reports on heart disease, the number one killer in America today. What impressed me as I watched the series was how easy it is to have a heart attack. We don't have to do anything to have heart trouble. Destroying our hearts is one of the easiest things in the world. All we have to do is sit back, relax, eat anything we want, and eat as much as we want, particularly of all that high fat, cholesterol-loaded junk food. Take it easy. We don't have to sweat, strain, or get any exercise. We can sit down in our armchairs, a sandwich in one hand, a cold drink in the other and watch television. We can keep on smoking, too. We don't have to do anything to have a heart attack. It's easy; it's the broad way, and it leads to destruction.

But there is also a narrow way. It's tough to watch our diet. It's tough to monitor how much we eat. It's tough to get the right kind of exercise. It's tough work to put that discipline into our lifestyle. It's hard work to stop smoking. It's the narrow way, but it's the way that leads toward life.

Jesus says it's like this in our relationship with God. There's a broad way, but it's the narrow way that leads to life. It's tough to study the Bible; it's tough to learn to pray; it's tough to put spiritual discipline into our life. It's a hard, narrow way, and there are not very many people who find it, but it's the way that leads to life. Jesus tells us that we can expect a growing relationship with God to lead toward life.

Another thing we can expect is that this relationship with God is going to give us strength. Matthew concludes with the parable of the wise and foolish builders. Jesus says, "Anyone who hears my words and does them is a wise builder. Anyone who hears my words and doesn't do them is a foolish builder." The choice is not, as we so often think, between good people and bad people. It is between wise people and stupid people. It's wise to follow Jesus' word and it's stupid not to. If we hear his words and do them, it's like building our house on the rock. The winds are going to come, the floods are going to rise, the storms are going to blow, but the house will stand firm. Hearing his words and not doing them is just like building our house on the sand. Sooner or later a hurricane is going to sweep up the beach and the whole thing is going to go down. Both builders hear the same word; both face the same storm, but one builder has found strength. Jesus doesn't promise escape from the storm, but he does promise that this kind of relationship with God will strengthen us to survive the storm, whole and complete in him.

Matthew ends this passage by saying, "When Jesus had finished these words the crowds were astonished, because he taught them (and he teaches us) as one who has authority."

Living into the Story
Suggestions for Reflection and Discussion

1. How would you say this description of our relationship with God differs from the common assumptions of that relationship in the world around us?

2. What does it mean to you to "practice your piety before men to be seen by them"?

3. Go back through the specific illustrations of the

personal nature of this unique relationship with God. How do they speak to your own experience?

4. What does it mean for you to call God "Father"? Do you have any problems with that term? What are the positive or negative emotions you feel about it?

5. What do you expect from your relationship with God? What are the tangible results you expect to see in your life as you grow in your faith?

7

What You See Is What You Get

Read: Matthew 8–11

Come with me in your imagination to the damp, clammy darkness of one of the prisons of Herod Antipas, notorious son of Herod the Great, ruler at Jesus' birth. Among the wretched, forgotten victims of Herod Antipas's jealousy, we find John the Baptist, waiting for his inevitable sentence, waiting to die. This rugged man of the wilderness, who lived with his face to the wind and the sky for a ceiling, is now confined to the lonely shadows of a dungeon cell. The "voice crying in the wilderness" sends out this anguish-filled question to Jesus, "Are you the One who is to come or shall we expect another?"

I feel John saying, "Jesus, I can almost make it, I can die in peace and allow the world to think I was a failure, if only I know for sure that you are the One whose shoes I am not worthy to unlatch, the One who is bringing in the kingdom of God. Are you the One? Or do we have to wait for another?"

It is a powerful plea, a desperate question. But Jesus does not answer it directly. Instead he says, "Go and tell John what you hear and see. The blind recover their sight, the lame walk, the lepers are made clean, the deaf hear, the dead are raised to life, the poor are hearing the good news, and happy is any man who doesn't find me to be a stumbling block." Tell John what's been happening around here and see if it doesn't look like the kingdom of God. What you see is what you get.

Here is what John could have seen. In chapters 8 and 9, Matthew draws together a marvelous collection of people whose lives have been touched by Jesus. He marches them out in front of us as if to ask, "Now, what does this look like to you?"

Chapter 8 opens with the story of a leper who says, "Jesus, I know if you want to you can make me clean." Jesus says, "Want to? You've got to be kidding! Of course I want to. Be clean!"

Next is a soldier, a Roman official, whose servant is paralyzed and in great pain. Jesus says, "I'll come to your house." But the centurion replies "No, Jesus, I'm not good enough for you to come to my house. But I am a man with authority over many soldiers and I know that if I give the word, they will do what I say. I know you can do the same." Jesus says, "Wow, I've never seen that kind of faith anywhere before." And that day, the Bible says, the servant recovered.

Next Peter takes Jesus to see his mother-in-law who has been sick with a fever. Jesus takes her by the hand and she gets up and goes to work in the kitchen.

In no time we find the disciples out in a boat when a great storm whips up the sea. They wake Jesus, who is asleep in the bottom of the boat. He asks them, "What are you afraid of?" Given the circumstances, they must have thought it was a crazy question! But Jesus goes on, "Oh, you of little faith." He steps to the front of the boat and rebukes the waves.

Next in line are two madmen, totally insane, totally out of control. By the time Jesus is finished with them, they are calm, collected, and sane.

When Jesus and his disciples return to Capernaum, where they are living, a group of people bring a paralyzed man to Jesus. Aware of their faith, Jesus says to the man, "Get up and walk, your sins are forgiven." The religious authorities think they know blasphemy when they see it. "Who are you to forgive sins?" they ask. Jesus responds, "I did it only to prove to you that the Son of man has the authority on earth to forgive sins."

If all this weren't enough, Jesus gets himself into even more trouble. He has dinner with a crowd of reprobate tax collectors, the kind of individuals with whom "good people" don't associate. When the religious leaders see him with this crowd, they criticize him for it. But Jesus says, "It is the sick who have need of a physician. I came not to call those people who think they are righteous, but those people who know they are sinners."

An official of the synagogue is next to come to Jesus for help. He says, "My daughter has died, come with me." At this point, the narrative is interrupted by the beautiful story of the woman who believes that all she has to do is touch the hem of Jesus' garment and she would be made whole. She touches it, is healed, and Jesus says, "Your faith has healed you." There may be no magic in the hem of the garment, but there is tremendous power in her faith toward the One who is wearing it. When Jesus reaches the house of the Jewish leader, he tells those mourning for the girl that she is not dead, but only asleep. Jesus wakes her to new life.

On the way out of town, Jesus asks two blind men who came to him, "Do you believe that I have the power to heal you?" They say, "Yes," and suddenly they can see again.

Finally, Matthew ends this collection of miracles with the story of a speechless man to whom Jesus restores the gift of speech. All the onlookers respond in amazement, "Nothing like this has ever happened before!"

It is quite an assembly. Matthew parades them across our imagination, asking, "What does this look like to you? Doesn't it look a lot like the fulfillment of the kingdom of God?"

In his massive work *On Being a Christian*, renegade Roman Catholic theologian Hans Kung writes, "The kingdom of God is creation healed." The kingdom of God is creation healed, sane, in harmony, made whole. The kingdom of God cannot be confined to some corner of human personality which we call "spiritual life." It is God's rule, God's harmony, God's peace, experienced in every corner of life. It is creation healed, personally and socially, spiritually and physically, politically and relationally, in its institutions and in its structures, in every dimension. The kingdom is creation made whole. This passage tells what it looks like for the kingdom of God to come on earth as it is in heaven. What you see is what you get. The answer to John's question, "Are you the One or shall we look for another?" is that we will know him by the difference he makes in the human situation, by the wholeness he brings to broken lives, minds, bodies, and relationships. "God's wisdom . . . is shown to be true by its results" (11:19, TEV).

An unknown poet of the fifteenth century caught the spirit of this affirmation when he wrote:

> Thou shalt know him when he comes,
> Not by any din of drums,

Nor the vantage of his airs,
Nor by anything he wears,
Neither by his crown,
Nor by his gown;
For his presence known shall be,
By the holy harmony
Which his coming makes in thee.

Matthew says, "Jesus went about all the cities and villages, teaching in their synagogues and preaching the gospel of the kingdom, and healing every disease and every infirmity" (9:35, RSV). The problem, obviously, is that Jesus could only be in one town or village; he could only teach in one synagogue; he could only heal one person at a time. Matthew records, "When he saw the crowds, he had compassion for them, because they were harassed and helpless, like sheep without a shepherd" (9:36, RSV). In order to expand the ministry, to extend the kingdom beyond the reach of his own hands, Matthew records, Jesus called his twelve disciples to him "and gave them authority to cast out unclean spirits and to cure every kind of ailment and disease" (10:1, NEB). He said to them, "Proclaim the message: 'The kingdom of Heaven is upon you.' Heal the sick, raise the dead, cleanse lepers, cast out devils" (10:7–8, NEB). In short, Jesus entrusts into the hands of these very human, very ordinary disciples the gift of the kingdom, and they become the extension of his healing in the world.

Who among us could walk through the towns and cities of our world and not be moved with compassion as Jesus is? Who among us can look at the suffering and pain, the oppression and injustice, the greed and bigotry of our world and not be moved with compassion? The amazing thing is that Jesus gives us, as his twentieth-century disciples, the authority to do something about all that suffering and pain. He gives us the authority in our world to be who he has been, to try to do what he tried to do. We can bring to bear on the kingdoms of this world the power and authority of the kingdom of God. The most amazing thing I know about the kingdom of God is that Jesus entrusts it into our hands! He gives us authority to be the extension of his healing presence in our world.

Let me give you a down-home illustration of how that works. The congregation of which I am a part defines its mission as being a "healing community" where persons experience "wholeness in their lives and relationships." Several years ago a woman came to Florida on the heels of a very painful, destructive divorce. Her self-esteem had been shattered, her confidence had been broken. In many ways coming to Florida was an escape from all of the pain behind her. She came into our congregation and got involved in the life of our church. Along the way she became a part of a small group for prayer and sharing. I remember the day she came to me and said, "Jim, for the first time in my life I heard somebody pray for me by name!" They listened to her, they absorbed her pain, they shared her struggles, they affirmed her hopes. Not long ago she left us and went back to that world of which she was so afraid, now strong enough to face it again. In a few weeks I received a letter from her in which she said, "I don't know what I ever would have done without that church!"

This is what can happen when the kingdom of God is entrusted into our hands to help us be about the business of bringing healing to lives and relationships, of raising dead hopes into new life, of breaking through the paralysis of shattered dreams, of casting out the demons of fear, injustice, greed, selfishness, and pride. This is what it means for Jesus Christ to give us the authority of the kingdom of God.

How is the kingdom realized in your life and in mine? How do we become part of that healing power in our world? The answer is faith, but not faith that floats off into some kind of mystical nirvana. Faith, instead, is concrete. It means living our lives under the authority of the kingdom of God revealed in Jesus Christ. When he says, "Go," we'll go; when he says, "Come," we'll come; when he says, "Do this," we'll do it.

This is the point of the story of the Roman officer who said to Jesus, "My servant is paralyzed and in pain. All you have to do is say the word and he'll be made whole." He goes on to explain what he means, "I, too, am a man under authority. I say to one soldier 'Go' and he goes, I say to another soldier, 'Come' and he comes. I say to my servant 'Do this' and he does it." Jesus was amazed and said to all of the people, "Never before have I seen such faith as this!"

The Roman centurion lived under authority. We all know that kind of authority; we all serve under a supervisor of some kind. Someday, that supervisor, whether a religious leader or an official in an office or corporation, is going to say, "It's time to go," and we'll go. This is a part of the agreement we have with our employer. This is also what Matthew means by faith. Faith is the choice to live under the authority of Jesus Christ. Faith means we choose to place our lives, our relationships, our values, our attitudes under the control and authority of Jesus Christ.

In spite of all my optimism, I find that I often expect the worst. When a friend said that she and her husband wanted to talk with me about a personal matter over lunch, I immediately thought, "Oh, no! I hope they aren't headed for a divorce!" Thankfully, it was nothing like that. They told me that he had been offered a new job, possibly a major step up in his career, that meant an undesired move to California. He said, "I've faced this kind of thing before, made the decision, and gone on. A year ago I probably would have accepted without thinking about it, certainly without thinking about God. But things have really changed since we got involved in the church. For the first time we are both asking what God wants us to do. Our faith is a new factor in the equation."

They have become people under a new authority, a man and woman who are learning to live by faith, learning to allow the spirit of God to guide the most significant choices of their lives. This is faith. It's the kind of faith Jesus saw in the centurian, the kind of faith that opens the possibility of being a part of the kingdom's fulfillment in our world.

Matthew concludes this section of his Gospel with an invitation offered by Jesus to all who would follow him: "Come to me, all who labor and are heavy laden, and I will give you rest. Take my yoke upon you" (11:28–29, RSV). In our day and our language this means get into the harness, put your shoulder into the work of the kingdom, put your life on the line to live out the authority of Jesus Christ in this world. "Take my yoke upon you and learn of me, for my yoke is good, my burden will be 'right' for you to bear."

Living into the Story
Suggestions for Reflection and Discussion

1. Put yourself in the position of the imprisoned John the Baptist. How would you feel? What would you be thinking?

2. If you were John and asked this question of Jesus, how would you feel about his response?

3. Take a close look at each of the people Matthew describes in this passage. How can you identify with any of them?

4. How do we experience the kingdom in our lives? What would be the evidence for you that Jesus was the One John promised?

5. Have you ever been a part of a fellowhip that experienced what it means to have the kingdom entrusted into their hands? How did that feel? What did you do?

6. What does the word *faith* mean to you? How does the story of the centurion illuminate new meanings for that word?

7. Use the words of the fifteenth-century poet ("Thou shalt know him . . . ") as a focus for your meditation and prayer.

8

Receptivity to the Kingdom

Read: Matthew 13:1–46

We began our study of Matthew by saying that the theme of his Gospel could be wrapped up in one question, "What will we do with the child born to be King?" Will we fall down and worship him like the Wise Men, offering him the best gifts of our lives? Or will we join Herod in a futile attempt to reject and destroy him?

The tension involved in this choice flows beneath the entire Gospel. By the time we get to chapters 12 and 13, the conflict begins breaking through the surface. The religious leaders make their choice. "The Pharisees . . . took counsel against him, how to destroy him" (12:14, RSV).

If I had been one of the disciples and had become aware of the tension, I think I would have asked, "What's going on here? If we're so good, why are we doing so poorly? If Jesus has such 'good news,' why are all the important people rejecting him?" Like Charlie Brown, I'd wonder how we could lose when we are so sincere. Jesus' answer is simple: "They look but they don't really see."

Flannery O'Connor, the south Georgia novelist, was a semi-invalid, confined to her home, where she raised peacocks. One day when a repairman came to the farm, she invited him to stop his work to watch the peacocks in the barnyard. As always, she was enthralled with their beauty. She described how "the bird turned slightly to the right and the little planets above him hung in bronze, then he turned to the left and they were hung in green." As the peacocks walked away she asked the repairman, "Well, what do you think of that?" to which he responded, "Never saw such long ugly legs! I bet that rascal could outrun a bus!"

Some people look and look, but they just don't see. Others, Jesus said, "Listen, but they don't really hear."

Bishop Gerald Kennedy used to tell about a time he arrived in a city for a preaching engagement. Tired and exhausted, all he really wanted was some peace and quiet before the services began. He had just settled into his hotel room when he heard the screeching of a violin in the room next door. He was about to complain to the violinist when the maid said, "Aren't you lucky! You get to hear Jascha Heifetz play and you don't even have to buy a ticket!"

Sometimes we listen, but we just don't hear.

Jesus said, "Their minds are dull," flat, insensitive, unresponsive. "They have closed off their ears and their eyes, because if they should see with their eyes and hear with their ears and understand with their heart, then they would have to turn to me to heal them."

The toughest problem Jesus faced in trying to communicate the meaning of the kingdom of God was limited receptivity. I would not call it spiritual blindness, but rather "spiritual myopia," nearsightedness. A dictionary defines myopia as a defect in which images are focused in front of instead of directly on the retina. That's what we try to do, isn't it? We try to keep the focus of the Gospel "out there" somewhere, out in front of us, at arm's length, rather than allow the words of Jesus to be focused directly into the retina of our lives and souls.

I never cease to be amazed at the unbelieveable lengths to which we will go to soften the tough demands of the gospel, to make it fit our presuppositions, to avoid applying it directly to our world and our lives. We look but do not see; we listen but do not hear.

Jesus describes this principle in a very earthy, simple parable. A sower went out to sow, and with the extravagance of the heavenly Creator who sends sun on the just and the unjust and rain on the good and the bad, he casts the seed, the message of the kingdom, into the world around him.

"Some," Jesus says, "fell on the path, where birds came and ate it." Some people are so impervious, so hardened by life, so set in their own ways that their souls are about as receptive as dried concrete and the seed never really has a chance to get in. We've made up our minds; don't confuse us with facts!

"Some," he says, "fell on rocky ground, where there was very little soil. These people hear the message gladly, but it doesn't sink deeply into them. When trouble comes they give up immediately." Deep down inside, they are shallow. The rolls of every church I know are loaded with the names of people who are like that. They come on strong at first, but there is no depth to their commitment, no spiritual root growing in them, and when the going gets rough, they drop off like flies.

"Then," Jesus continues, "some of the seed fell in and around thorns." They get off to a good start, but the thorns grow faster than the seeds. These people hear, but worldly cares and love of riches choke the message. Upton Sinclair said that it is difficult to get people to understand something when their salary depends on not understanding it. Nothing chokes our understanding of the gospel as quickly as the realization that our love of riches depends on not understanding it. The problem is not that the Christian faith has been tried and found wanting, but that it has been tried and found difficult.

But Jesus also says, "Some seed fell onto good soil." The odds seem to be about one in four. These hearers' eyes are clear, their ears are open, and they are like rich, freshly plowed soil. The seed sinks deep into them where it grows, slowly, almost imperceptibly at first, until it brings a great harvest, greater than anyone expected; thirty, sixty, one hundredfold.

The easiest thing to do with this parable is to ask, "What kind of soil am I?" That's where I started. But as I submitted my own life to the scrutiny of this passage, I realized that it is not this simple. We do not fall into one of these categories and stay there. All of us fall into some of these categories some of the time. One area of my personality may be open, receptive, like freshly plowed soil, while another may be as impervious as concrete. On one issue I may see clearly what Christ expects of me, but on another I may be as blind as a bat and as deaf as a brass monkey.

At a major conference on the Holocaust, I heard Dr. Franklin Littell relate the story of a trip he made to Germany in the early 1930s. He visited with the Methodist bishop in Germany, who told him how bad things had been, but that now there was a leader who was turning things around. He was restoring pride in the nation and discipline to the young, and was rebuilding the economy. The words seared into Littell's memory when the bishop said, "Hitler is God's man for Germany."

When Littell told the story, he said with tears in his voice, "Remember, the bishop was a good man, a very good man." But he, like thousands of other good people, was blind to the evils of the Third Reich.

It is easy to point fingers at German Christians in Nazi Germany, but let us not forget that, for most of the first century of the American nation, there were thousands of good people, profoundly committed Christians, who saw no conflict between their commitment to Christ and their commitment to slavery. I must not forget that several years before Fort Sumter, the Methodist Episcopal Church split in two over that issue. It was 1939 before we were reunited. And even as late as Easter, 1964, a black bishop, Charles F. Golden, was denied entrance to a white Methodist church in Jackson, Mississippi.

Spiritual myopia is a very tricky business. There were Christians in Germany, and there were men and women across the history of this nation, who had eyes to see and ears to hear the message of the kingdom; men and women who bore witness to the truth when others were blind.

Perhaps our problem as human beings is that we are victimized by bigness. We think the important things are all large, loud, obvious, and noisy. But Jesus said the kingdom comes like a tiny mustard seed planted in the ground, growing into a great tree. The kingdom comes like yeast, mixed into the dough and permeating the whole. The kingdom comes like a gift of loaves and fishes which seems insignificant at the time, but is used to feed five thousand people.

The kingdom is like a treasure hidden in a field, buried beneath all the noise and confusion of our world, but he who finds it runs off in joy and sells all he has to buy that field. It is like a fine pearl, lost amid the junk of a village flea market, but every now and then someone recognizes its worth and sells all he has to buy it.

One of my personal spiritual heroes is E. Stanley Jones. In his spiritual autobiography, *A Song of Ascents*, he tells the story of the day he looked at his own life and realized what had made the difference for him.

I gasp in surprise and wonder. Life is working and working with rhythm and joy. How did it all happen? I asked myself that question as I sat in a hotel room in Alaska writing. I looked up and saw myself in a looking glass and said to myself: "Stanley Jones, you're a very happy man, aren't you?" I replied, "Yes, I am." And then the vital question: "How did you get this way?" And my reply: "I don't know. It is all a surprise to me, a growing surprise. I walked across a field one day, and I stubbed my toe against the edge of a treasure chest, jutting out of the earth. 'It's treasure,' I cried. Ran off and sold all I had, including myself, and bought that field; and I've been hugging myself ever since that I had sense enough to do it.

No wonder the message Jesus preached was always the same: "The kingdom of God is at hand." For those with eyes to see and ears to hear, the kingdom is all around, within our grasp, if only we will receive it and give it a chance to grow!

In chapter 20, the story of the last miracle before Jesus' final journey to the cross goes like this:

Two blind men who were sitting by the road heard that Jesus was passing by, so they began to shout, "Son of David! Have mercy on us!"

The crowd scolded them and told them to be

quiet. But they shouted even more loudly, "Son of David! Have mercy on us!"

Jesus stopped and called them. "What do you want me to do for you?" he asked them.

"Sir," they answered, "we want you to give us our sight!"

Jesus had pity on them and touched their eyes; at once they were able to see, and they followed him.

—Matthew 20:30–34, TEV

The Christ who caused blind men to see promises to open our eyes and open our ears, if only we will allow it.

Living into the Story
Suggestions for Reflection and Discussion

1. Jesus said, "They look but they don't see; they listen but they don't hear." Have there been times in your life when these words described what was happening to you? Be specific. What was it that you saw but didn't see or heard but didn't really hear? How did you come to that realization?

2. Have you ever experienced "spiritual myopia" as defined here? Have you tried to keep the words of Jesus out there, at arm's length, rather than apply them to the core of your life?

3. Look again at the parable of the seed and the soils. Assuming that all of us can identify with each of the "soils" at different times in our spiritual journey, which kind of soil best describes your receptivity to the message of the kingdom right now? Why?

4. What would it mean in your life today for Jesus to give you the ability to see, as he did for the blind beggers?

5. Spend at least five minutes in silent receptivity to the spirit of Christ. Be still and allow your mind to be open to whatever images, thoughts, or impressions might come from the living presence of Christ.

9

Along the Way of the Cross

Read: Matthew 16:21–20:28

Most of the United Methodist preachers in Florida had gathered for the first annual Institute of Preaching. It was a major event featuring world-famous speakers. The bishop was presiding with appropriate dignity, trying to keep everything running smoothly. At the beginning of one worship service he announced that the leaders were to meet the photographer to take pictures for the conference archives. He said, "Immediately following the benediction, please meet me at . . . " His mind went blank and it was obvious that he had absolutely no idea where they were to meet. He stammered for a moment and finally said, "Just look for me at the end of the service. By then I'll know where I am going."

The speaker who followed him observed that some sermons are confused in the same way. Sometimes the preacher seems to be asking the congregation to come on board with no idea where he is going. Some lives are like that, too. Some of us live in quiet confusion, with absolutely no idea of where life is headed or where it will come out.

What a contrast that lack of direction is to the picture Matthew paints of Jesus! Reading through the Gospels reminds me of a quote I heard while I was in junior high school. The idea echoes the teachings of Jesus: The world will step aside to let us pass if we know where we are going.

Jesus says, "I know where I am going. I know where this is going to end. If I am to be the Messiah, if I am to be faithful to the call of God in my life, if I am to fulfill the promise of the kingdom of God, I must go to Jerusalem, there to suffer, be put to death, and, on the third day, rise."

This sense of direction, of calling, is so strong that when Peter protests, "God forbid that should ever happen to you!" Jesus responds with these harsh words, "Get away from me, Satan! You are an obstacle in my way, because these thoughts of yours don't come from God, but from man" (16:23, TEV). Three times in chapters 16–20 Jesus announces clearly where he is going, and three times the response of those around him is totally inappropriate.

The first announcement of the cross is in the context of Jesus' call to discipleship. If someone asked me for one verse that captures what it means to be a Christian, I would quote this verse: "If any man would come after me, let him deny himself and take up his cross and follow me. For whoever would save his life will lose it, and whoever loses his life for my sake will find it" (16:24–25, RSV).

One morning while I was visiting a condominium on the Gulf of Mexico, a person staying in the unit above me began throwing bread crumbs out over the balcony for the sea gulls. They seemed to come out of nowhere, swooping down to catch the bread crumbs in midair. But there was a stiff wind blowing in off the gulf. I watched as the gulls would literally hurl themselves into the wind, allow the wind to carry them back, then hurl themselves into the wind again. It seems to me that Jesus is saying we only find life when we hurl ourselves into the wind. The ones who would save life, hold it tightly, protect it, will lose it. But the ones who hurl themselves into life, will find it.

Martin Niemöller died in 1984 at the age of ninety-two. When the Nazis began to take over he was at first passive, like most Christians in Germany. But as time went by, he could see the direction the movement was going. As a pastor in Berlin, he stood directly in their path. They banned him from preaching, but he ignored their ban. They arrested him. He was sent to prison, then to Dachau. Across the forty years following the war, he has been one of the strongest Christian leaders in Europe. He lived life to the hilt, and at ninety-two was still working, still witnessing, still proclaiming the gospel. He had found something worth giving his life to—he hurled himself in the wind.

Matthew's second announcement of the cross comes in 17:22–23: "When the disciples all came together in Galilee, Jesus said to them, 'The Son of Man is about to be handed over to men who will kill him; but three days later he will be raised to life.' The disciples became very sad" (TEV).

Being sad did not help them understand what Jesus was saying. Right on the heels of this, in chapter 18, they ask a question which reveals all too clearly how far they are from understanding what the cross means. "Who is the greatest in the Kingdom of heaven?" (18:1, TEV). The question itself reveals that they do not know. In response, "Jesus called a child, had him stand in front of them, and said, 'I assure you that unless you change and become like children, you will never enter the Kingdom of heaven. The greatest in the Kingdom of heaven is the one who humbles himself and becomes like this child'" (18:2–3, TEV). Jesus is explaining the way of humility. We have a tough time with that word *humility*, just as we have problems with the term *self-denial*. When the Bible talks about humility it doesn't mean artificial self-depreciation; it doesn't mean we should live with a neurotic inferiority complex; it doesn't mean we should say, "O, what a worm am I." Humility simply means that no one swaggers into the kingdom, chest puffed out, self-pride glowing. No one comes into the kingdom shouting, "Here I am, Lord, just the one you need to clean up this mess. God, are you ever lucky to have me!" The only way into the kingdom is the narrow way, the way of self-surrender, the way of forgiveness, the way of humility.

In chapter 19, Matthew records a repeat performance of this scene. People are bringing children to Jesus. The disciples, impressed with the importance of their discipleship, scold them and tell them to take the children away. But Jesus says, "Let the children come to me, and do not hinder them; for to such belongs the kingdom of heaven" (v. 14, RSV). In the very next passage, verses 16 through 22, just to make sure we don't miss the point, Matthew paints a stark contrast with the story of the rich young man who has everything and comes to Jesus asking, "Master, what do I have to do to gain eternal life, life that is really alive, life that is more than mere existence, life like I've seen in you?"

Jesus says, "Keep God's commandments if you want to enter into life."

The young man looks at Jesus and responds, "Lord, I've kept all those since my youth!"

Jesus, looking deeply into the young man's soul, says, "Well then, let's try this one. Go, sell all you have and give it to the poor, then come follow me. Get rid of your pride, your power, your prestige, your wealth, all the things that protect you from facing up to who you really are. Get rid of all the externals and then come, just as you are, and follow me." Matthew records that the young man went away very sad because he had great riches.

There is only one way into the kingdom—the way of childlike humility, the way of one who prays:

> Just as I am, without one plea,
> But that thy blood was shed for me,
> And that thou bidst me come to thee,
> O Lamb of God, I come, I come!
> Just as I am, poor, wretched, blind;
> Sight, riches, healing of the mind,
> Yea, all I need, in thee to find,
> O Lamb of God, I come, I come!
> Just as I am, thy love unknown
> Hath broken every barrier down;
> Now, to be thine, yea, thine alone,
> O Lamb of God, I come, I come!

The third announcement of the cross is set in the context of the disturbing story of the mother of James and John. Matthew said she comes to Jesus asking for a favor. "Promise me that when you come as king these two sons of mine will sit at your right and left hand."

Jesus replies to them, "You don't know what you're asking. In the first place, it's not mine to give. It is not my kingdom, it is the kingdom of God, and only God decides who belongs where. And in the second place, are you able to drink the cup that I am to drink?" With almost unbelievable naivete, they say, "Yes, Lord, we are able."

Jesus then describes what it means to drink that

cup: "You know that the rulers of the heathen have power over them, and the leaders have complete authority. This, however, is not the way it shall be among you. If one of you wants to be great, he must be the servant of the rest; and if one of you wants to be first, he must be your slave—like the Son of Man, who did not come to be served, but to serve and to give his life to redeem many people" (20:25–28, TEV).

The way Jesus is going is the way of servanthood, the way of loving, caring, joyful, costly self-giving for others. Frankly, this is a theme that is conspicuously absent from most of the pop, cultural, and political Christianity in America today.

The last parable Matthew records before Jesus' death is the parable of the final judgment. One day the Son of Man is going to be recognized as the King, and he is going to be seated on a royal throne with all the nations of the world before him. He will divide them into two groups, the sheep and the goats. And the King will say to the ones on his right, "Come blessed of my Father, inherit the kingdom prepared for you. For I was hungry and you gave me food, thirsty and you gave me a drink, a stranger and you received me, naked and you clothed me, sick and you took care of me, in prison and you visited me." And the sheep are going to say, "Lord, when did we see you hungry, or thirsty, or naked, or sick, or in prison?" And the King will say, "Inasmuch as you did it for one of the least of these, my brothers and sisters, you did it for me."

Then he is going to turn to the ones on the left and say, "Depart from me! I was hungry and you didn't feed me, thirsty and you didn't give me a drink, naked and you didn't clothe me, sick and you didn't care for me, in prison and you didn't visit me, a stranger and you didn't receive me." They will say exactly the same words the sheep said, "Lord, when did we see you hungry and not feed, thirsty and not give you a drink, naked and not clothe you?" And the King will say to them, "Inasmuch as you did not do it for one of the least of these, my brothers and sisters, you did not do it for me" (25:31–45).

There is no doubt about where Jesus is going; he has set his face to go to Jerusalem. It is the way of self-surrender, the way of humility, the way of servanthood. In short, it is the way of the cross, and he invites us to follow him.

Living into the Story
Suggestions for Reflection and Discussion

1. Have you known people who "live in quiet confusion, with absolutely no idea of where life is headed"? When have you experienced that lack of direction in your life?

2. In contrast, have you known people who clearly knew where they were going? When have you known that sense of inner direction?

3. Jesus says that if we try to save our lives, we will eventually lose them. If we willingly lose our lives for the sake of a greater goal, we will find them. Do you agree? How have you seen that principle worked out in real-life situations?

4. What does humility mean to you? How important is this idea in your life?

5. How do you picture the concept of "servanthood"? What emotions do you experience when you hear or read the story of the final judgment? Do you identify with the sheep or the goats?

6. What changes would need to be made in your life if you seriously began to follow the way of the cross?

Can you share some of them with others in your group and ask them to pray for you?

7. Conclude your time of sharing by focusing on the words of "Just as I Am."

10

Love—Rejected or Received?

Read: Matthew 21:1–22:14, 23:37–39

We began this journey with an old man gazing into a portrait by Karsh, hearing the music of Pablo Casals. Perhaps the only way we can hear the music of this section of the Gospel is to gaze into one of the most poignant pictures of Jesus anywhere in the New Testament. "The child born to be King" is coming to Jerusalem, the center of authority and of faith. Along the way the crowds have cheered, "Praise be the one who comes in the name of the Lord!" throwing down their palm branches, but Jesus knows where all this is going to lead. He knows the way that began at Bethlehem will end at Calvary. He knows the road, although lined with cheering crowds, will end at the cross. He knows that the voices, which at one moment cry out their acceptance and their praise, will in the end shout rejection and call for his death.

Matthew's portrait captures him on the Mount of Olives, looking out over Jerusalem. You can hear the tears choke his voice as he says, "Oh, Jerusalem, Jerusalem, how often I would have put my arms around all of your people, like a hen gathering her chicks under her wings, if you had let me. So your Temple will be abandoned, your streets will be empty and you'll not see me anymore."

William Barclay titles this passage "the poignant tragedy of rejected love." It is the gripping portrait of the One who would wrap his arms around his people but is rejected.

Have you ever tried to give someone a hug and had them turn you away? Has there been a time you went to a child, but most likely to an adult, with the sheer intent of expressing your love, your friendship, your respect and offered a hug only to be pushed off with an elbow? I have a friend who has a fascinating way of shaking hands. He offers you his hand, but you get his elbow. The body language is fascinating. No one gets close to him, no one really knows him very well because the body language is clear: "You can come just this far, but I won't let you in."

Jesus said, "Oh, how I would have wrapped my arms around all your people, but you wouldn't let me." This is a central part of the drama of Matthew. Jesus offers love and life, but the people turn him away.

John captured this theme in his Gospel in one verse: "He came unto his own, and his own received him not" (John 1:11, KJV). He came to his own at that time, and he comes to us today, not in the power of a kingly palace but in the humility of a stable; not riding on the back of a great white Roman stallion, the symbol of power and authority but on the back of a donkey, the symbol of servanthood and simplicity. He comes not to be served but to serve and to give his life as a ransom for many. He comes not with power that subdues but with love that frees. He comes to his own with nothing more than sheer sacrificial love, which would bring healing, hope, freedom, and joy.

He comes to his own and, all too often, his own receive him not.

Jesus teaches this lesson in a powerful parable, one of the clearest pictures we have of the meaning of his coming. It is also a psychologically accurate picture of your experience and mine. Jesus says there was a farmer who planted a vineyard, dug a well, and put a wall around it. He turned the vineyard over to the tenant farmers and gave them everything they could have wanted, but the vineyard still belonged to him. The harvest time came and the owner sent his servants to gather the harvest. But when the tenants saw the servants coming they beat them, killed them, and threw them out. This happened over and over again until finally the owner said, "I will send my son; surely they'll respect him." But when the tenants saw the son coming, they said, "Let's kill him and have his property for our own." So they jumped him, tossed him out of the vineyard, and killed him.

Jesus said to all the people standing around, "When the owner of the vineyard comes back, what is he going to do to those tenants?"

The crowd responded, "He'll kill those evil men and rent the vineyard to someone who will pay him his share of the vineyard when it is due."

Jesus concluded the parable by saying, "The stone which the builders rejected has become the main corner-stone" (21:42, NEB).

This is a tough parable, not nearly as pleasant as some of the others, but it is terribly accurate. Love is offered to us and when we reject that love, when we turn it away, we become hard, insensitive, and self-destructive.

Later, Jesus points his finger at the Pharisees, saying, "You are like whitewashed tombs! On the outside you look sparkling clean but on the inside you are full of dry bones and rotting flesh" (23:27).

On the outside you look human, real, as if you would be able to respond to people around you, but on the inside you are cold, hard, and dead. This is what happens when we reject the gift of love.

Not long ago I heard the tragic story of a man who, after his father's death, confided with a friend that he would remember his father primarily as a man balancing himself on top of a huge mound of ice. The mountain raised him above other people, but at the same time it trapped him. Whenever he would consider the possibility of coming down off his perch, one look at the slipperiness of the slope would discourage him. Furthermore, if he did come off that mountain, he would be just like everyone else, sharing their weakness and their humanity. He lived his life up there, isolated from human relationships, praying that the dark and cold would keep his mountain intact, cursing the sunlight of human love which kept trying to melt it all away.

This is a tragic picture of rejected love. So tragic, in fact, that the Son of God weeps over it, saying, "Oh, how I would have taken you into my arms, but you would not let me."

The Gospel of John, however, does not leave us with tragedy. John does not only say, "He came unto his own, and his own received him not," but goes on to say, "But as many as received him, to them gave he power to become the sons of God" (John 1:12, KJV). To as many as receive the gift, to as many as allow the love of God to wrap itself around them, to as many as receive him he gives the power to become what God has always intended, the sons and daughters of God. The shocking message of the Gospel is that you and I have nothing we can contribute to our salvation except our receptivity. There is no way I can make myself good enough, noble enough, attractive enough, and talented enough to earn God's love and favor. I can only receive it as a free gift of his grace, totally undeserved, totally unearned, totally unre-payable—the gift of his love.

We preach this, sing it, affirm it, talk it, but we have difficulty living it! At least I know that it is difficult for me to live as if I know that I am accepted and loved by the infinite grace of God. This is given not on the basis of anything I achieve or merit, but solely because God has it in his being to love me, to love this world, and to love you. God is like that mother hen who wants to hold her chicks under her wings, if only they will let her.

This is one of the lessons Jesus teaches in his next parable. He says the kingdom of heaven is like a man who sent out invitations for a wedding feast. No one came to the feast and the house was empty. The man went to his servants and said, "My house must be full. Go out into the streets and gather up every warm body you can find and bring them into the wedding party." That's how you and I got in! The great dragnet of God's love is dragged through the streets and it picks up people like us. All we can do is allow him to wrap his arms around us in infinite love.

This is a difficult message for us. We would like to be able to do something to deserve such treatment. It's difficult for us to realize that all we can do is receive. I remember a "Twilight Zone" episode that starts out with a character who is obviously a "self-made man," one who controls his destiny and his world. We see him in his office, in all his strength and power.

He leaves his office, drives off, and is in a tragic automobile accident. The tragedy is that he is totally paralyzed, except for one index finger. The emergency crew thinks he is dead. From here on we see the story from his perspective. The voices around him are saying, "Don't worry about him; he's already dead. Take care of the rest." But all the time this confident, self-made man is self-assured, saying, "Not to worry, I'll take care of this, I have it under control." He can still move his finger.

The emergency crew loads him in an ambulance and takes him off to the hospital. All the time he is still confident, still thinking he can control his fate. At the hospital they put him on a rolling cart. He can move his finger, so under the sheet he begins to tap his finger on the metal bar. But there is a thump on the tire on that rolling bed and as the bed rolls down the hall the thump keeps perfect time with his finger. His message is missed. It goes unheard. Finally, at the end of the show, they are rolling him up to the morgue. As the attendants are ready to pull the sheet over his head, one of them says, "Wait! This one isn't dead yet; there's a tear in his eye."

It is tough for us to realize there is nothing we can do but receive the gift, perhaps with a tear in our eye. The only thing we can contribute to our salvation is our receptivity. But the promise is that to all who accept the gift he gives power to become sons and daughters of God.

What a powerful portrait of Jesus, looking out over the city of Jerusalem, looking into your life and mine, saying, "How I would wrap my arms around you if only you will let me."

Living into the Story
Suggestions for Reflection and Discussion

1. Begin with a few moments to silently capture the picture of Jesus weeping over the city in your imagination. What emotions are in this picture?

2. Have you ever offered love and been rejected? What emotions did you feel?

3. The parable of the vineyard is one of the lesser known and "harder" parables of Jesus. How do you respond to this interpretation of it? Do you accept the idea that it is an accurate psychological description of what happens to us when we reject love?

4. What does it mean to "receive him"? Have you ever experienced the "power to become sons and daughters of God"?

5. Most of the time we experience the love of God through the love of others. Is there someone you need to wrap in your arms of love? How can you share that love with others and thereby discover it for yourself?

11

Jesus Is Coming Again— So What?

Read: Matthew 24:36–25:13

Comedian Joan Rivers has a one liner that I like to use now and then. She uses it when she breaks into her machine-gun-like monologue asking, "Can we talk?" This means, "Can I really be honest with you?"

Can we talk?—about one of the most difficult and sometimes confusing affirmations of our faith? Matthew 24–26 leads us head-on into what theologians call "eschatology," meaning "end things" or "final things." More popularly we refer to it as the "second coming," though you will not find that particular term anywhere in the Bible. This concept is affirmed in the Nicene Creed: "He shall come again with glory, to judge both the quick and the dead." Can we talk about the final coming of Christ?

Let's begin with the obvious observation that "final coming" speculation is big business these days.

Hal Lindsay's *Late Great Planet Earth* has sold 15 million copies. When James Watt, a former secretary of the interior, was questioned on the long-term effects of his environmental policies, he suggested that it did not matter, as Jesus may be returning soon.

Some of the TV evangelists are having a field day with the subject. I heard one go through a long discussion of premillennialism vs postmillennialism vs amillennialism, only to conclude that he had it right and all the rest were wrong.

There is a lot of discussion on this subject in our daily lives, as well. I recently asked our senior high youth what they wanted to know about the Bible. They asked me about the book of Revelation. They had heard a lot of talk at school about "the mark of the beast," the end of the world, and all the rest.

"Can we talk?" When I read some of these pulpy paperbacks, listen to some of the TV sermons, see some of the bumper stickers, and hold it all up against what the Gospels actually say, I am reminded of a book title I saw some time ago. A book of quotations by Jean Arbeiter is entitled *No Matter How You Slice It, It's Still Baloney.* No matter how thin you slice it, a lot of what is said about the final coming sounds like baloney to me.

In all this talk about the "end times," however, there are two affirmations of which I am absolutely sure.

Affirmation number one: History is going somewhere. It is going toward the fulfillment of the kingdom of God. This is the shorthand way of saying that Jesus is coming again.

The bottom line of biblical faith is the confidence that human history is more than a meaningless cycle endlessly repeating itself, more than a chaotic assortment of meaningless events. History is moving toward a grand finale, a great climax. When the last scene is played and the curtain falls, "every knee will bow and every tongue confess that Jesus Christ is Lord." God is constantly at work in history to fulfill the kingdom that has already been revealed in Jesus Christ. All of human life and history will confirm that

Jesus is right, that the way revealed in him is the way life and history are meant to be completed.

One of my favorite pieces of music is the *1812 Overture*. I love the way Tchaikovsky introduces the basic theme at the beginning of the piece and weaves it through, sneaking it in here, just a hint of it there, almost lost in the cacophony at one point, until he comes to that final movement when the entire orchestra and chorus, complete with booming cannon, bring the theme to its full, resounding conclusion.

My understanding of human history is like the *1812 Overture*. Every now and then, in the midst of all the confusion of life, we hear the music, catch a glimpse of the kingdom revealed in Christ, and know that at the end of time the grand theme will be fulfilled when "the kingdom of the world has become the kingdom of our Lord and of his Christ, and he shall reign for ever and ever" (Rev. 11:15, RSV).

I can't explain this; it's mystery to me. Frankly, the people I doubt the most are the ones who are most confident that they have it all together. But I am certain that history is moving toward the fulfillment of the kingdom of God. Jesus is coming again.

Affirmation number two: No one knows when this is going to happen. When I hear people trying to second-guess the Bible, to figure out all the images, to chart the time and the place that Jesus will come again, I have two reactions. First, I am reminded that church history is littered with well-intentioned people who have predicted his coming in the past, missing it entirely. In every age there have been sincere people of faith, along with a good percentage of kooks, crooks, and three-dollar bills, who have said, "This time we've got it right! This time we've figured it all out. We know he's coming now!" My first reaction is that we've heard all this before. It sounds like the little boy crying wolf.

My second reaction is to ask, "Haven't you read the Bible?" In these passages, there are many things open to interpretation, but there is one thing that Jesus says so clearly we have to be blind to miss it: "No one knows . . . when that day and hour will come—neither the angels in heaven nor the Son; the Father alone knows" (24:36, TEV). None of us knows the time, therefore all of us are called to live every day as the "Day of the Lord." If we knew the date, most of us would sit around waiting to cram for our exam!

Several years ago there was a 105-year-old man in Leesburg, Florida. When asked to what he attributed his longevity, the man replied, "If I'd known I was going to live so long I'd have taken better care of myself." There is something of this in all of us. The point of Jesus' warning is that we are called to live every day, every moment, in the awareness of the coming of the kingdom of God. No one knows the time. We should all live every day in anticipation of the kingdom coming on earth as in heaven.

These are my affirmations: Jesus is coming again, and no one knows the time. But then the question becomes, so what? What are the implications of these affirmations for our lives today? Jesus has two clear words for us.

The first of these is, "Keep awake!" Jesus says, "Watch out. . . . You . . . must always be ready, because the Son of Man will come at an hour when you are not expecting him"(24:42, 44, TEV). To underline the point, Matthew records the parable of the five wise and five foolish virgins.

Jesus says the coming of the kingdom will be like ten virgins or bridesmaids, waiting for the bridegroom to come and take them all to the celebration. Five, he said, were wise and brought extra oil for their lamps. Five were foolish and didn't. The bridegroom was later than they expected and they fell asleep.

About midnight the cry went out, "The bridegroom is coming. Trim your lamps and come to meet him." By this time, the lamps had burned down and needed more oil. The foolish maidens ran to the marketplace to get oil, but while they were gone the bridegroom came, took the others inside, and closed the door. When the foolish bridesmaids tried to get in, the bridegroom said, "I don't know you," and they were shut out. Jesus concludes by saying, "Watch out, then, because you do not know the day or the hour" (25:13, TEV).

Plodding my way through William Manchester's biography of Churchill, I learned a number of things about World War I. Britain's greatest blunder of the war happened in the Dardanelles, that narrow strait of water in Turkey that connects the Aegean Sea to the Sea of Marmara and Constantinople.

Churchill recommended that the British navy, the greatest fleet in the world, sail up the Dardanelles, take Constantinople, and end the war. On March 18, 1915, the invasion began. The first day went perfectly but at the end of that day, largely out of fear of the risk and danger ahead, the admirals decided, against Churchill's recommendation, to pull back and take a more cautious approach. Historians all agree that this resulted in a missed opportunity, which allowed the war to go on for three more years.

Ten years after the aborted invasion, Roger Keys, one of the admirals, sailed up the narrows into Constantinople. When he arrived, he said, "My God, it would have been even easier than I thought! We simply couldn't have failed . . . and because we didn't try, another million lives were thrown away and the war went on for another three years." The British missed their opportunity, and the consequences were horrendous.

Jesus is saying to us, "Keep awake! Always be

prepared to seize your opportunity, to grasp the moment, to experience the joy of the kingdom when it comes."

The second application is, "Always be working." This is not a prescription for workaholics, but a call to be faithful to our task as the people of the kingdom, the disciples of Jesus Christ.

Matthew records Jesus asking a question: "Who, then, is a faithful and wise servant?" The disciples are concerned about when the end is going to come, but, for Jesus, the critical questions seem to be, "What are you doing in the meantime? Who is the faithful and wise servant?" Then Jesus answers his own question: "Happy that servant who is found at his task when his master comes!" (24:46, NEB).

We are not called to figure out when the end will come. We are not called to interpret all the images and symbols which fill the pages of Daniel and Revelation. We are not called to determine who will be in and who will be out of the kingdom. We are simply called to be at our task, to be faithful to the work God has given us to do, to be a part of the coming of the kingdom in our world.

This message is consistent throughout every one of the parables and stories the Gospel writers record about the final coming. The pattern is always the same. A master puts his servants in charge of his property and goes on a trip. He comes back to check things out and the servants who have been faithful to their trust, who have used what they were given wisely and well, are the ones who are rewarded. But the ones who have abused their trust and squandered their gifts are cast out.

"Happy," Jesus said, "[is] that servant who is found at his task when his master comes!" (24:46, NEB).

Gary Blonston was a forty-one-year-old reporter

for the *Detroit Free Press* when he discovered he had cancer. He shares his feelings, his choices, his reaction to the reality which suddenly stood up hard and cold before him in these words.

> Before we learned that my cancer was confined to my eye, I had spun the calendar forward, imaging what life would be like if the doctors told us it had a known end point. How would we live? Would we try to end with a flourish, take the dream trip—East Africa, New Zealand, the Grand Tour? Or would we live as before, savoring our lives as they have been—good, solid, loving lives?
>
> Suddenly I understood those big-money lottery winners who say, "Aw shucks, we'll still be just the same folks as before." To be sure, we felt like the opposite of lottery winners, but the reflexes seemed the same. There would be no dream trip for us. It would be unnatural, strained, unlike us. It would not serve as any sort of escape but simply as a nagging reminder of why we were doing it."
>
> In the time left, we would live as we have lived, the way we know how, regardless of outcomes and end points. We would be us, most likely. There was some comfort in that. Nothing could touch our center, even this.

His words describe the spirit with which I believe Jesus expects us to respond to the reality of his final coming. "Happy is the servant who is found at her task when her master comes."

There was a nameless Negro slave who discovered this faith in the final coming of Christ and put it in these words:

> There's a king and a captain high,
> And he's coming by and by,
> And he'll find me hoeing cotton when he comes.
> You can hear his legions charging in the regions
>   of the sky,

And he'll find me hoeing cotton when he comes.
There's a man they thrust aside,
Who was tortured till he died,
And he'll find me hoeing cotton when he comes.
He was hated and rejected,
He was scorned and crucified,
And he'll find me hoeing cotton when he comes.
When he comes! When he comes!
He'll be crowned by saints and angels
    when he comes.
They'll be shouting out Hosanna! to the man
    that men denied,
And I'll kneel among my cotton when he comes.

Living into the Story
Suggestions for Reflection and Discussion

1. What is your most honest reaction to the idea of the Second Coming? Excitement? Disbelief? Fear? Confusion? Confidence? Skepticism?

2. What difference does it make in your life to believe that "history is going somewhere"? Does the analogy of the *1812* Overture have practical meaning for your faith and experience?

3. How would you apply the parable of the wise and foolish virgins to your own experience? What opportunities have you missed because you were not watching your life closely enough?

4. If you were Gary Blonston—forty-one years old with cancer—how would your response differ from his?

5. Some things need to be heard and felt rather than read. Read "When He Comes" out loud, catching the feeling of the spiritual. Can it become a basic affirmation of your faith?

12

A Last Supper
That Still Lives

Read: Matthew 26:6–30

Leonardo da Vinci's masterpiece, *The Last Supper*, is one of the most famous paintings of all time. Some art critics call it the greatest masterpiece of the Renaissance. The artist has frozen in time that moment when Jesus said, "One of you will betray me" (26:23, NEB). He did this by plumbing a psychological depth that no other artist had ever reached. Andrew's hands are thrown up before him in shock. Judas clutches his bag of coins. Thomas, with one finger in the air, is asking, "Which one, Lord?"

Five centuries of weather, dirt, war, sheer human stupidity, and attempts at restoration have done their worst. It is now called "the most abused masterpiece in the world" and at some places Leonardo's work is entirely lost. Currently, however, the most extensive restoration project ever attempted is under way. Dr. Pinin Brambilla Barcilon, working with a microscope and the skill of a surgeon, is carefully, painstakingly, peeling away five centuries of dirt, mold, and paint, to get down to the real Leonardo. According to

National Geographic, the goal of the restoration is to preserve for future generations a *Last Supper* that still lives.

As I studied Matthew's narrative of Jesus' Passover meal, it occurred to me that perhaps it needs a similar kind of radical surgery. Beneath the accumulated layers of history, theology, debate, and sometimes sheer boredom which surround the Sacrament, we need to rediscover the living reality, the vitality of what Jesus did in the upper room. We need to rediscover a Last Supper that still lives as a vibrant reality in our experience.

Matthew, as a skillful artist, uses comparison throughout his narrative. He holds one picture, one event, one parable up against another, casting new light on both. He does that in chapter 26. In the same frame as his picture of the Last Supper, he places a picture of the dinner party in Simon's house, telling of a nameless woman who came to the party bringing an alabaster jar of expensive perfume.

Just before Christmas, my wife and I were walking through the mall and came upon a well-dressed woman handing out free samples of after-shave lotion. Not a person to pass up a free gift, I took one and I tried it. It was very nice. I told my wife that if she wanted something to put in my stocking, she could pick up a bottle of that after-shave. A couple of weeks later, she came in from a shopping trip and said, "Forget it, Sweetheart. The cologne costs forty-five dollars an ounce! I'd call that caviar taste on a peanut butter budget!"

That was expensive perfume, but it was cheap compared to what this woman brought. According to Mark and John, the cost of the perfume was more than would have been needed to feed the 5,000 people Jesus fed with the loaves and fishes. She brought her perfume, broke the bottle, and poured it on Jesus' head. It was the expression of profound love, deep respect, abiding honor.

When the disciples see it, Matthew says, they become angry, saying "What a waste! This could have been sold and the money given to the poor." I've often wondered what they actually would have done if they had had the money. Theoretical generosity is always in the extreme. It's amazing how generous people can be when they don't have anything to give.

Jesus responds, "Don't bother her. She has done a beautiful thing, like preparing me for burial. And everywhere the gospel is proclaimed, this story will be told in memory of her."

Jesus is not giving a lecture on the economics of poverty, much less justifying greed or self-indulgence in the face of glaring need. The focus is on this woman and her act of extravagant, irrational, costly love. Matthew is holding this picture up beside the picture of the Last Supper to say, "Look at the extravagant love of God, who loves the world so much that he gives his son! This bread is his body, broken like her alabaster jar for you. This cup is his blood, poured out like her priceless perfume for you." At the center of the Last Supper, at the center of the Gospel, is the extravagant, irrational, undeserved, unearned love of God.

The Last Supper still lives in our experience of that extravagant love given to us by God in Jesus Christ. It still lives in every expression of extravagant, costly love we give to each other in his spirit.

As I thought about this woman, I thought of other women I have known. One called me on Christmas Eve, the first Christmas our church family celebrated in our own building. She asked if I would stop by that afternoon. Her husband, a semi-invalid, had never been inside the building. I made my way to their modest home. When I got there she told me that they had been saving for several years, hoping to build a house on a piece of land they owned in North Carolina. Now, she said, it was obvious they were never going to be able to do that and she wanted me to put the money in the Christmas offering, instead. From her dresser drawer she pulled out ten one hundred dollar bills. That Christmas Eve I placed her gift in the offering as an expression of their extravagant, irrational love for Christ and the church.

The "Christmas Freeze" occurred in Florida in 1983. It was cold! On Christmas morning, another woman met me at the church door with a special glow on her face. She said she had good news. She had sold her fur coat and wanted to put the money in the Christmas offering. It was her gift of extravagant, remarkable love for Christ.

It doesn't only happen at Christmas, and it doesn't only happen with money. Visiting in the home of some friends in another community, I met their aunt, Tish. I don't know how old Aunt Tish is, but I suspect she won't see eighty again. Her husband died many years ago and she has moved into a two-room apartment next door to my friends. As they showed me around her apartment, they pointed out the furniture that her husband, a woodworker, had built by hand. The bed, the dining table, the end table, the chair; he had built them all. Then they showed me his masterpiece. It was a copy of Leonardo da Vinci's *Last Supper*, not painted in oils, but carved out of tiny slivers of wood. Every detail was there in different colors and textures of wood, carefully glued together to form the masterpiece.

I tried to imagine the infinite hours, the tremendous skill and patience which went into that work. I realized that it was his gift of extravagant love, not only for the Lord who is at the center of the carving, but also for her. It still lives as the expression of that love.

Commenting on the woman with the jar of perfume, Jesus said, "Everywhere the gospel is proclaimed the stories of people like these will be told in memory of them." The Last Supper still lives in the extravagant love of God in Jesus Christ and in every expression of love we give to each other in his spirit.

One of the legends concerning why it took so long for Leonardo to finish his painting is that he walked through the streets of Milan searching for faces for the disciples. He would find Matthew in a market, Thaddaeus in a cafe, Peter in a mill. He would memorize the line of each face and then return to the refectory wall to paint those details into the disciples' faces.

I wonder how it would have felt to have been one of those villagers and to walk into that dining hall to discover yourself painted into the Last Supper, seated at the table with Jesus? That is precisely what we are invited to do each time we share the Sacrament: to find ourselves around that table, to feel again the extravagant love of God given to us in the broken body and poured out blood of Jesus Christ our Lord, and then to find ways to share that extravagant love with others. In that way, the Last Supper still lives!

Living into the Story
Suggestions for Reflection and Discussion

1. Find a a copy of Leonardo da Vinci's *Last Supper.* Study the expressions on the faces of the disciples around the table, the position of their bodies, the emotion which the artist captures there. What do you find that you never saw before?

2. How have you experienced the extravagant love of God which the Sacrament represents?

3. Have you ever wanted to give an extravagant expression of love to someone else as the woman did for Jesus? How did it feel? What did you do?

4. Can you remember some experiences of Holy Communion when the meaning of the Sacrament came alive for you? How did it happen?

5. Meditate on these words by Horatius Bonar.

> Here, O my Lord, I see thee face to face;
> Here would I touch and handle things unseen,
> Here grasp with firmer hand eternal grace,
> And all my weariness upon thee lean.
> . . . .
> Too soon we rise: the symbols disappear;
> The feast, though not the love, is past and gone.
> The bread and wine remove: but thou art here,
> Nearer than ever, still my shield and sun.

13

When the Going Gets Tough

Read: Matthew 26:36–66, Psalm 42

What do you do when the going gets tough? How do you respond when the world tumbles in around you? When you feel betrayed by a best friend? When all your fondest dreams and highest hopes are shattered like crystal on the floor? When you've struggled with tough decisions and hardly know which way to turn? When the future looks so ominous that it scares you to death? What do you do when the going gets tough?

Our high school football coach hung slogans and signs all around the locker room to crank everybody up and get the team all excited. There was one right by the door where we came in from the field that read, "When the going gets tough, the tough get going." It didn't help much—I think the team finished the season with one win out of eight games—but it was a good idea. He must have read the same books as Robert Schuller. One of his recent best-sellers is titled *Tough Times Never Last, But Tough People Do!* I think this is true, although my experience tells me that sometimes it is a dead heat and a photo finish to see whether the times are going to outlast the people or the people are going to outlast the times.

This passage in Matthew's Gospel is where the going gets tough. The dark clouds are starting to close in, all the powers of evil are mounting their last offensive, all of the predictions that Jesus made about his suffering and his death are beginning to come true. The questons we have to ask are, What did Jesus do? How did Jesus cope when the going got tough?

Matthew records that after the Last Supper Jesus and his disciples go out to the Mount of Olives where Jesus says, "All of you, this night, will leave me and run away, for the scripture [Zech. 13:7] says, 'Kill the shepherd and the sheep will be scattered.'" Jesus begins his facing of tough times with a strong dose of realism. There is no dodging the issue, no pretending it doesn't exist, no flight of fancy into a world with no pain.

Several years ago I participated in a workshop led by Lyle Schaller, the country's foremost authority in church leadership, growth, and development. In the opening session, Schaller said that one of the goals for the workshop was for us to learn how to say, "Naturally." We would be able to look at a situation and say, "This is normal, predictable human behavior. Given the circumstances and given who we are, this is just what we should expect. Naturally." This ability has been very helpful to me. When I run into some problem, some conflict in the church, I can lean back and say, "Naturally. I should have expected that. Given who we are, given the circumstances, that's normal, predictable human behavior."

It seems to me Schaller described Jesus' response very clearly. Given the circumstances, given the people with whom he had to work, this was normal, predictable behavior. "All of you are going to run away and leave me." That's realism.

As you read through the Passion narratives, you will find that these events are loaded with very real, very normal, very predictable human emotions. This is the stuff of your life and mine. Jesus says to the disciples, "My heart is so weighted down with grief and sorrow that it almost crushes me." We understand this. All of us face those moments of grief and disappointment which weigh heavily upon us and almost crush the life out of us.

We can hear Jesus struggle in prayer with God, searching for some other way through: "Father, if there is any way possible to get me out of this mess, get me out of it!" There are times in all our lives when, confronted by the circumstances and realities around us, we cry out, "God, give me an escape hatch! Get me out of this!" Jesus experiences this with us.

The disciples are jarred awake from their restless sleep as a crowd with swords and clubs breaks the silence of the garden. They watch as Judas kisses Jesus, forever becoming the symbol of betrayed trust, broken friendship, and shattered loyalty. We can compare our own feelings when we have felt the searing pain of betrayal.

We can feel the anger boiling up in those disciples, the desire to strike back, to get even. Matthew says one of the disciples (John tells us it is Peter) draws his sword and slashes off the ear of the High Priest's servant. Jesus responds, "Put away your sword. Those who live by the sword die by the sword." Jesus understands that we cannot overcome evil with more evil. All this can do is compound the total amount of evil in the world. In John, Jesus heals the ear which was severed, demonstrating that the only way to overcome evil in this world is with good.

Peter follows at a distance as Jesus goes to trial. Unable to find anything against Jesus, the council of priests and elders brings in lying witnesses to slander him. There is something in all of us that cries out, "That's unfair! It's unjust!"

Through it all, we empathize with Jesus. We also feel the desperate loneliness, the utter desolation, as all the disciples flee and run away. Those who had promised to be loyal to death are gone. We must remember that this is all exactly what Jesus expected, exactly what he saw coming. It is as if Jesus looked at all of that natural, predictable human behavior and said, "Naturally. That's the kind of world we live in. That's what it means to be human."

This is the real substance of your life and of mine. There are no simple answers for it. The Gospel offers no easy way out. The Gospel does not promise that, if we pray about it, it will go away, like taking two aspirin and waking up feeling better in the morning. In fact, Jesus prayed about it and things got a good deal worse! There are no simple solutions to tough times in the Gospel. Instead, the Gospel offers us hope. Everytime Jesus predicts the coming of the cross he also predicts the coming of the resurrection. In this passage, when Jesus realistically says, "All of you are going to leave me and run away," he also says, "but when I am raised to new life, I will go before you in Galilee." That's hope!

It is fascinating that at this point in the story there is absolutely no evidence to support that hope. Such hope is based solely in Jesus' confidence that God is at work in his life and that God will see him through the tough times to new life. It is the kind of hope Job had. He lost everything except his confidence in God. In the middle of all of his suffering, he was able to say, "Though he slay me, yet will I trust in him" (Job 13:15, KJV). It was Job who said, "I know that my Redeemer liveth, and that he shall stand at the latter day . . . and though . . . worms destroy this body, yet in my flesh shall I see God" (Job 19:25–26, KJV). We sing these words on Easter, on the other side of the empty tomb, but Job sang them in the face of death, as darkness closed in around him. That's hope!

This is the kind of hope Paul had when he wrote to the Roman Christians, who at any moment could be dragged out to the Colosseum and fed to the lions:

> I consider that the sufferings of this present time are not worth comparing with the glory that is to be revealed to us. . . . For in this hope we were saved. Now hope that is seen is not hope. For who hopes for what he sees? But if we hope for what we do not see, we wait for it with patience. . . . We know that in everything God works for good with those who love him, who are called according to his purpose (Rom. 8:18, 24–25, 28, RSV).

Paul concludes this magnificent chapter with a great crescendo: In all of these predictable, human circumstances, "we are more than conquerors through him who loved us . . . . [Nothing] will be able to separate us from the love of God in Christ Jesus our Lord" (Rom. 8:37, 39, RSV). That's hope!

This is the hope that a Jew had, scrawling these words on the basement wall of a German home before being carried away to a concentration camp: "I believe in the sun even when it isn't shining; I believe in love even when I can't feel it; I believe in God even when he is silent." That's hope!

This is the hope I shared with a woman who had experienced all the terrors of hell in her life. She said it felt as if the powers of darkness were just about to overtake her. Everytime she got up on her feet something would come along and knock her over again. But she said to me, "I am beginning to feel that I'm going to get better." That's hope!

This is the same hope expressed by the writer of Psalm 42. He says his sorrow and suffering are like waves that thunder over him, like a waterfall that is about to crush him. The writer cries out the words which Matthew records Jesus saying on the cross, "My God, why have you forsaken me?" (v. 9). But the psalmist goes on to say, "Why art thou cast down, O my soul? and why art thou disquieted within me? hope thou in God: I shall yet praise him" (v. 11, KJV). That's hope!

Gutzon Borglum, who carved the faces of the four presidents on Mount Rushmore, heard Merton S. Rice preach on that, "Yet Shall I Praise Him", at Metropolitian Methodist Church in Detroit during the time he was working on the memorial. He was so moved by the text and the sermon that, out of the stone of Mount Rushmore, he carved a statue as a gift to Merton Rice. Borglum's statue now stands in the courtyard of Metropolitan Methodist Church. It is the figure of a young man who has obviously been through very tough times. His shirt has been torn from his back and hangs in shreds around his waist. Behind him is the form of a dragon, the sculptor's image of the conflict and struggle through which this young man has come. His face is turned upward so it can hardly be seen from the ground. But, from the second floor of the Education Building, looking down into the courtyard, the viewer can see directly into the young man's face. He is smiling—not a cheap, superficial smile, but a smile of deep inner confidence and hope. The young man appears to face the circumstances around him in confident assurance that he shall live again. Borglum carved in the base of the statue those words: "I shall YET praise him." That's hope!

Living into the Story
Suggestions for Reflection and Discussion

1. Think back across your life to some of the most difficult times you have faced. Try to get in touch with your emotions, your feelings, and how you responded to the "tough times."

2. Can you think of times in your life when it would have been helpful to say, "Naturally"? How does a good dose of realism help you face difficult times?

3. Use your imagination to put yourself into each of the events in this part of the Passion story. How would you have felt if you had been there during the garden prayer? If you had received Judas's kiss? If you had seen the trial? Would you have run away?

4. How would you define "hope" in your own experience? Can you identify with any of the illustrations of hope included here?

5. Read Psalm 42 in the King James Version and then compare it to a contemporary translation. What kind of faith comes across to you?

14

What Shall I Do with King Jesus?

Read: Matthew 27:1–2, 11–54

Choices. The events of Palm Sunday and Holy Week are, like the events of your life and mine, all about choices. The words originally belonged to Robert Frost, but they have become so much a part of our national heritage that now they belong to all of us:

> Two roads diverged in a yellow wood,
> And sorry I could not travel both
> ....
> I took the one less traveled by,
> And that has made all the difference.

The Gospel is all about choices, too—choices which made all the difference.

We have been following the story of Jesus, as recorded in Matthew, from Christmas to Easter, from birth to glory. We observed the way Matthew records the Christmas story, turning the spotlight on Herod and his bloody slaughter of the baby boys in Bethlehem, a jealous king's futile attempt to destroy the child born to be King. Matthew tells the contrasting story of the Wise Men from the East who found the child, recognized him for who he was, offered him their gifts, and went home a different way. They made their choice, and it made all the difference.

Through Matthew's narrative we watched "the child born to be King" grow into a man. We saw his life and now know what the kingdom, the rule of God, looks like in real human flesh and experience. We heard his words and now know what he expects of us, what it will cost to follow him. We felt his spirit and now know the power of God's love, mercy, compassion, and peace revealed in him.

Finally, in the closing scenes of the drama, Matthew replays his opening theme. This time the spotlight is on Pilate, the Roman Governor in Jerusalem, and his tortured struggle with this question: What shall I do with Jesus called the Messiah?

It is early Friday morning. Jesus, the One who set others free, is brought before Pilate in chains. Pilate asks him directly, "Are you the King of the Jews?" Are you who they say you are? Are you the One who reveals God's rule, God's way, God's kingdom in human life? And Jesus answers, "That's what you say."

The Living Bible paraphrases Jesus' answer as yes, but that is not what Matthew records and it is not what he means. Jesus is hurling the question right back into Pilate's lap, just as he did when he looked into the eyes of the disciples and asked, "Who do you say that I am?" (16:15, RSV). The choice is up to Pilate, as it is to each of us. The kingdom of God is not imposed from without but realized from within. The kingdom comes on earth as it is in heaven not by political force or military power, but by the inner conviction of men and women who have experienced God's rule in Jesus Christ and have chosen to follow him. The kingdom comes through a community of men and women who choose to live their lives in faithfulness to Jesus Christ. The choice is up to us.

Pilate really does not want to deal with this, so he goes out to the crowd and plays a round of "Let's Make a Deal." "Which one do you want me to set free for you? Jesus Barabbas or Jesus called the Messiah?" (27:17, TEV).

Matthew does not tell us very much about Barabbas. The other Gospel writers say he was a bandit, a murderer, an insurrectionist. I hear Pilate saying, "Who would you rather have roaming around in your world? Jesus Barabbas or Jesus of Nazareth? With whom would you rather have to deal? The bandit, the murderer, the insurrectionist or the Prince of Peace?" And Matthew records that the whole crowd made the choice, "Give us Barabbas!"

There was a time in my life when I thought theirs was a strange response, but I've grown older and wiser to the ways of the world. It doesn't surprise me anymore. One of my favorite Easter plays is a chancel drama entitled "Christ in the Concrete City." At this point the dramatist has the crowd shout back at Pilate:

Give us Barabbas, his ways are our ways.
Give us Barabbas, we understand him.
And he understands us. Good old Barabbas! Our lives are not condemned by his holiness, not like this other.
Give us the murderer. We want Barabbas!

Is it possible that our world still knows better how to deal with a bandit, a murderer, an insurrectionist than it knows what to do with the Prince of Peace? There is a sense in which an assassin's attempt on the pope's life is less shocking to our world than the pope's forgiveness of him. Is it possible that we would rather deal with raw power that rides on a stallion than with this one who comes on a donkey, with the weapons of love, patience, suffering, and peace? Given the choice, isn't it possible that we would take Barabbas, too?

Pilate is in a bind. The crowd is shouting for Jesus' death. With the skill of every politician before and since, he gives the crowd exactly what they want, takes his basin, and tries to wash his hands of the whole bloody mess. It won't work, of course. At least the crowd, however, has enough good, common sense to shout back, "Let the responsibility be on us!" They knew the truth that Pilate tried to ignore, namely, that we are responsible for our choices in this world. We can choose our actions, but we will live with the consequences of those actions. The road we choose will determine our destination, and that choice will make all the difference.

The rest of this story is familiar to us. We know how the soldiers beat Jesus until the flesh was torn from his back. We know how they mocked him and called him "king." We know how they humiliated him and marched him through the city until his bloody body was no longer able to carry the crossbar to Golgotha. We know how they nailed him to the cross. We know the only words Matthew records from his parched, dying lips: "My God, my God, why hast thou forsaken me?" (27:46, RSV). And we know how he gave a loud cry, breathed his last, and died.

But we should notice the characters Matthew sneaks on stage in the closing scene. Like those wise men who showed up in Bethlehem, we don't know their names, we don't know where they came from, we don't know how many there were. All we know is that an army officer and some soldiers were assigned to watch Jesus die. But Matthew records that when they saw everything that happened, they said, "He really was the Son of God!" (27:54, TEV).

It seems that Matthew uses them in the same way that he used the Wise Men in the opening of the Gospel, to hurl the choice out there in front of us, to force us to ask: Will we be like Pilate and Herod, the ones who had all the evidence, but who chose to reject his way, deny his truth, and ultimately, to wash their hands of the whole mess? Or will we be like those wise men who saw nothing more than a baby in his mother's arms, or those soliders who saw nothing more than the bloody body of a dying man, but who recognized him for who he was and who, from the depths of their souls, said, "Truly this was the Son of God!" (27:54, RSV).

Pilate was in a difficult position. The choice was forced upon him: he had to do something with Jesus. I suspect that the rest of his life was marked by that choice. It was likely that way for the Wise Men, who, Matthew records, went home from Bethlehem by a different way. Though we never hear of them another time, it is safe to assume that their lives could never be the same again.

It will probably be that way in your life and mine. Matthew forces the choice upon us, not once, but over and over again in the daily patterns of our lives: What will we do with Jesus at this time? In this situation? In this relationship? Will we ignore him, reject him, attempt to wash our hands of him, and go our way? Or will we love him, obey him, live with him, follow him, claim him as the Christ, our King? What will you do with Jesus who is called the King?

> I shall be telling this with a sigh
> Somewhere ages and ages hence:
> Two roads diverged in a wood, and I—
> I took the one less traveled by,
> And that has made all the difference.

Living into the Story
Suggestions for Reflection and Discussion

1. Have you ever stood at the place where two or more roads diverged in your life? How did you make your choice?

2. Compare the characters of Herod and Pilate. How are they alike? How are they different?

3. Read through Matthew's account of the crucifixion (Matt. 27:27-54). If you are in a group, have one of the members read the story aloud to give the full impact of it. What catches your attention? What have you never noticed before?

4. In Matthew 27, circle or underline each time the word "King" or "Messiah" is used. How does Matthew's emphasis on the Kingship of Jesus speak to your faith?

5. If you have access to the recording, listen to "The Crucifixion" from *Jesus Christ, Superstar* by Webber and Rice. Share with someone the impact it has on you.

6. Prayer focus:

> Holy Spirit, Right divine,
> King within my conscience reign;
> Be my Lord, and I shall be
> Firmly bound, forever free.
> —Samuel Longfellow

15

King Forever!

Read: Matthew 27:57–28:20

How would you end the story which Matthew began in Bethlehem? How would you conclude the story of this child who was born to be King? After walking through the life of Jesus as Matthew has presented it, after viewing all the pictures Matthew has hung on the walls of our imagination, there is a sense in which the events of chapters 27 and 28 are the only logical conclusion to the story. There is really no other way it could end.

The powers which tried to deny and destroy Jesus are still at work, even after his death. The chief priests and Pharisees combine with Pilate to seal the tomb, making it as secure as is humanly possible. They leave behind soldiers, representatives of Roman power, to guard it.

For Matthew, the sealing of the tomb is the final picture of just how far the powers of death and darkness will go to deny the kingdom of God. It can be the end for the kings of earth, but not the end for the kingdom of God.

As the sun rises on Sunday morning, Matthew

records, a sudden earthquake jolts the area. An angel of the Lord descends from heaven, his face shining like lightning, his garments white as snow. With the full power of heaven, he breaks the seal of the powers of earth, scatters the military power of Rome, defeats the power of death, rolls back the stone, and sits down on it like a victorious general relaxing after the battle which won the war.

At the end, just as at the beginning, Matthew's narrative is different from the other Gospels. Mark, Luke, and John never attempt to describe the actual opening of the tomb. They tell the story from the perspective of those who discovered the empty tomb with the stone already rolled away. Only Matthew attempts to describe the event itself.

Why? We may find an answer if we see this final picture in a frame with the rest of the Gospel. Once again, Matthew is drawing the conflict between the authority of the kingdoms of the world and the authority of the kingdom of God in Jesus Christ. In one dramatic image, he is saying that the powers which stand in opposition to the rule, will, and way of God revealed in Jesus, though they may triumph for a time, will ultimately be overwhelmed, scattered, and destroyed. You can nail this Jesus to the cross and seal his body in a tomb, but ultimately you cannot deny his truth, reject his authority, or obliterate his presence. Here is the Technicolor portrayal of the promise that "the kingdom of the world has become the kingdom of our Lord and of his Christ, and he shall reign for ever and ever" (Rev. 11:15, RSV)!

An old Latin hymn attempts to describe the truth which Matthew presents in picture form:

> The strife is o'er, the battle done;
> The victory of life is won;
> The song of triumph has begun:

Alleluia!
The powers of death have done their worst,
But Christ their legions hath dispersed;
Let shouts of holy joy outburst:
Alleluia!

Sometimes on Easter Sunday, I dream of being in Coventry Cathedral in England. Coventry is an industrial town, one of the first cities bombed by Hitler in World War II. The morning after the bombing, as the residents of Coventry emerged from their bomb shelters, their worst fears were confirmed. The magnificent Cathedral Church of St. Michael, which had stood at the center of the city since the Middle Ages, lay in rubble. Incendiary bombs had gutted the wooden rafters and roof. All that remained of the building were the smoke-stained stone walls.

Immediately after the war, the effort began to rebuild the cathedral, but instead of tearing down the ruins, the architects left them standing. Adjacent to them was built one of the most magnificent religious structures of the twentieth century. On Easter the worshippers at Coventry begin in the old cathedral, looking toward the ruins of the altar where the words "Father Forgive" are carved in stone. Then, they turn and move into the exuberant brightness of the new cathedral, where Christ is enthroned in majesty over the high altar in the largest tapestry in the world.

Coventry stands as the visual witness to the triumph of good over evil, the victory of life over death, the power of the kingdom of God over the power of the kingdoms of the earth. This is the victory Matthew proclaims in the grand finale of his Gospel.

The final picture in Matthew's gallery is of the risen, triumphant Christ on the mountain, his disciples prostrate before him, the light of a new dawn glowing in the sky, the glory of new life shining in his face. Here Matthew records his final words of victory: "All authority in heaven and on earth has been given to me" (28:18, RSV). It is the ultimate affirmation of faith in the kingdom of God. Paul expressed this confidence when he wrote these words to the Corinthian Christians (1 Cor. 15:24-27, NEB):

> Then comes the end, when he delivers up the kingdom to God the Father, after abolishing every kind of domination, authority, and power. For he is destined to reign until God has put all enemies under his feet; and the last enemy to be abolished is death.

The final pictures in Matthew's gospel are not only a bold affirmation of faith in the triumph of the kingdom of God, they are also a daring challenge to the disciples. The only logical response to this Gospel is the Great Commission:"Go into all the world and make disciples of all nations, for I am with you always, even to the end of time."

One of the most courageous witnesses for Christ in recent years was Archbishop Oscar Romero, the leader of the Roman Catholic Church in El Salvador, who was killed on March 24, 1980, while celebrating Mass in a hospital chapel in San Salvador.

With unflinching courage, he applied the message of liberation and justice to the political and social struggles of his homeland. In his last homily on March 23, he acknowledged "the risk that is run by our poor station for being the instrument and vehicle of truth and justice," but he went on to say that, in the context of the Lenten season, "all of this is preparation for our Easter, and Easter is a shout of victory. No one can extinguish that life which Christ revived. Not even death and hatred against him and against his Church will ever be able to overcome it. He is the victor!"

The next day, Oscar Romero was dead. The awesome powers of hate and oppression had done their worst. But Oscar Romero's witness still lives. His life and words have become a part of the coming of that kingdom which will ultimately prevail.

Christ is the victor. He is King forever, and those who recognize him, whether they be young or old, weak or strong, become his witnesses to the world, confident that the King is with them, even to the close of the age.

Living into the Story
Suggestions for Reflection and Discussion

1. What is your earliest memory of Easter? When and how did you first hear the story of the resurrection?

2. Have you ever thought of the resurrection story as "a Technicolor portrayal of the promise that 'the kingdom of the world has become the kingdom of our Lord and of his Christ'"? What does that affirmation mean to you?

3. The resurrection made couragous witnesses out of the first disciples. Oscar Romero is a comtemporary example of this courage. Have you known any people who shared this kind of witness? How did their confidence in the resurrection help or encourage them?

4. Look back across the entire sweep of this study. What scenes or stories spoke most clearly to you? Where did you experience the presence of Christ in your own life?

5. Close this study by meditating on the words of "The Strife Is O'er" or on the words of "Christ the Lord Is Risen Today."

James A. Harnish pastors St. Luke's United Methodist Church at Windermere, a congregation he helped to organize in 1979, in Orlando, Florida. He is actively involved in the civic and religious lives of his community.

He has served other United Methodist churches in Florida and has published in *The Upper Room Disciplines* and *Christian Home*. He and his wife Marsha have two daughters, Carrie Lynn and Deborah Jeanne. This is his first book.